The Acts of the Apostles

The Acts of the Apostles

Commentary on the Holy Scriptures of the New Testament

Volume II

Archbishop Averky (Taushev)

Translated from the Russian
by Nicholas Kotar

Edited by Vitaly Permiakov

Holy Trinity Seminary Press
Holy Trinity Monastery
Jordanville, New York

Printed with the blessing of His Eminence,
Metropolitan Hilarion First Hierarch
of the Russian Orthodox Church Outside of Russia

The Acts of the Apostles

HOLY TRINITY
SEMINARY PRESS

An imprint of

HOLY TRINITY PUBLICATIONS
Holy Trinity Monastery
Jordanville, New York 13361-0036
www.holytrinitypublications.com

ISBN: 978-1-942699-15-6 (hardback)
ISBN: 978-1-942699-16-3 (ePub)
ISBN: 978-1-942699-17-0 (Mobipocket)

Library of Congress Control Number 2017945139

Third Printing 2025

Printed in the United States of America
Books International, 22883 Quicksilver Dr, Dulles, VA, 20166
booksintl.com

Contents

For we cannot but speak the things which we have seen and heard.

(Acts 4:20)

For I have not shunned to declare to you the whole counsel of God.

(Acts 20:27)

For I think that God has displayed us, the apostles, last, as men condemned to death.

(1 Cor 4:9)

Therefore, brethren, stand fast and hold the traditions which you were taught, whether by word or our epistle.

(2 Thess 2:15)

Preface

First and foremost, it should be self-evident that I have used all of the exegetical works of the Holy Fathers, especially St John Chrysostom and Blessed Theophylact of Bulgaria, as well as the interpretations of Scripture (based on patristic sources) provided in the "Holy Trinity Periodical," published before the Revolution in Russia and "The Patristic Exegesis of the Gospel of Matthew," which was published by the journal *Eternal Things* and edited by Bishop Methodius these past few years in Paris, in three volumes.

Without aiming for any particular scholarly goals, I intend to give readers and those who study the New Testament a key to understanding and interpreting the Scriptures according to the teachings of the Orthodox Church. Such a handbook, considering the general scarcity of books and publications of this nature, could at least partially replace all the previous Russian pre-Revolutionary textbooks and guides. I beg the reader to be lenient in assessing my work because I never had the opportunity to wholeheartedly give myself to it, as such a lofty subject would require, and I worked on it only sporadically. Even for such an opportunity, I thank God, hoping that my work will not be without usefulness, and I ask every reader to pray for me.

—Archbishop Averky

Editor's Note: This text emerged from lecture notes. The translator and editors did not always have access to the same editions of the Russian language books used by the author. Furthermore, not all of these works exist in English translation, and in cases in which they do, it is not always possible to cite a corresponding reference. Additionally, the author followed a Russian cultural and intellectual practice in which it is not considered essential to give all details of the source material but simply an indication of its origins. Therefore, the sources and endnotes at the end of this English edition are listed only to facilitate the reader's understanding or indicate as closely as possible a source for further reading and study.

Introduction

This book is the second volume of the *Commentary on the Holy Scriptures of the New Testament.* The first volume concerned the four Gospels, and this current volume concerns the Acts of the Apostles. In the Russian, this section together with the Epistles of the New Testament is called by the traditional name of "Apostolos," because it contains the Acts and the writings of the apostles of Christ (including the fourteen Pauline Epistles and the seven General Epistles, as well as the Revelation of St John).

The material offered consists of a series of summary lectures for the course of the Holy Scriptures of the New Testament, which I taught at Holy Trinity Orthodox Seminary in Jordanville, New York, between 1952 and 1955.

Being a seminary lecture course, this overview relies heavily on such secondary works as the Commentary on the Apostolos by Bishop Michael (Luzin) (1830–1887), and the commentaries on the Pauline Epistles by St Theophan the Recluse, as well as on the collection of articles by Matvei Barsov (d. 1896) and several other pre-Revolutionary seminary textbooks, including those by Archpriest Michael Kheraskov (1836–1901), Alexander V. Ivanov (1837–1911), Archpriest Nicholas Alexandrov, and others.

This volume, like the first, has as its purpose the instruction of the word of God for all lovers of Scripture in the proper interpretation given it by the Holy Orthodox Church. This is especially necessary in America, where even among Orthodox Russians, the virulent preaching of Protestant sectarianism confuses many, turning them away from the right path.

I ask my readers to forgive all omissions and insufficiencies of this volume of my work, covering them with your love and prayers for my soul.

—Archbishop Averky
\+ March 31, 1976 (by the Old Calendar)

CHAPTER 1

The Meaning of the Term "Apostolos"

The second part of the New Testament consists of holy books that usually are united, at least in their liturgical usage, under the general term "Apostolos" (Апостол in Russian or ἀπόστολος in Greek). The word "Apostolos" means "messenger." This name was given to the disciples of the Lord Jesus Christ, sent by Him to preach the Gospel to all mankind. Just as the word "Gospels" now indicates the written word (originally the oral preaching) concerning the life and teaching of the Lord Jesus Christ, the word "Apostolos" refers to the extant writings of Christ's apostles, including their deeds, lives, and teachings. This division of the New Testament into two parts—the Gospel and the Apostolos—is of ancient provenance. We find this division and the name "Apostolos" in the writings of St Irenaeus of Lyons, Clement of Alexandria, and Tertullian.

The Content of the Apostolos

Even though in the first centuries of Christianity many books appeared bearing the title Acts, Epistles, and Revelation, the only authentic and canonically recognized books are the following (twenty-three in number):

1. The Acts of the Apostles
2. St Paul's Epistle to the Romans
3. St Paul's First Epistle to the Corinthians
4. St Paul's Second Epistle to the Corinthians
5. St Paul's Epistle to the Galatians
6. St Paul's Epistle to the Ephesians
7. St Paul's Epistle to the Philippians
8. St Paul's Epistle to the Colossians
9. St Paul's First Epistle to the Thessalonians
10. St Paul's Second Epistle to the Thessalonians
11. St Paul's First Epistle to Timothy

12. St Paul's Second Epistle to Timothy
13. St Paul's Epistle to Titus
14. St Paul's Epistle to Philemon
15. St Paul's Epistle to the Hebrews
16. The General Epistle of the Holy Apostle James
17. The First General Epistle of the Holy Apostle Peter
18. The Second General Epistle of the Holy Apostle Peter
19. The First General Epistle of the Holy Apostle John the Theologian
20. The Second General Epistle of the Holy Apostle John the Theologian
21. The Third General Epistle of the Holy Apostle John the Theologian
22. The General Epistle of the Holy Apostle Jude
23. The Book of Revelation (the Apocalypse) of St John the Theologian

In this collection of writings, Acts is a book of historical record, the Epistles of St Paul and the General Epistles are instructional in nature, and the Revelation of St John is a book of prophecy.

In his Thirty-Ninth Festal Epistle, St Athanasius of Alexandria also mentions that "there are other books besides these not indeed included in the Canon, but appointed by the Fathers to be read by those who newly join us, and who wish for instruction in the word of godliness." Among such books, he mentions the Didache (Teaching of the Twelve Apostles) and The Shepherd of Hermas. Aside from those books, St Athanasius mentions the so-called apocryphal (i.e., hidden, secret) books that are "invention(s) of heretics," who attribute them to the apostles, "so that, using them as ancient writings, they may find occasion to lead astray the simple." Following patristic witness, the Church rejects the pseudo-epigraphical (fabricated) and apocryphal (hidden, esoteric) books that claim apostolic origin but do not reflect the authentic apostolic doctrine. The faithful are discouraged from reading those books, as their reading can bring spiritual harm.

CHAPTER 2

Overview of the Acts of the Apostles

THE WRITER OF THE BOOK AND THE REASON FOR ITS COMPOSITION

The Book of the Acts of the Apostles, as is evident from its first few words, is a direct continuation of the Gospels. The author sets himself a goal to describe the events that occurred immediately following the ascension of the Lord Jesus Christ, and to give a summary of the establishment of Christ's Church on earth by the labors of the holy apostles, especially the Holy Apostles Peter and Paul. St John Chrysostom, in his first homily on Acts, describes in detail the great significance of this book for Christianity, as it confirms the truth of the Gospel with factual information from the lives of the apostles.

"This book," he says, "is mostly filled with proofs of the resurrection.... This is the content and most important purpose of this book." This is also why the faithful prepare themselves for the great feast of Pascha by reading the complete Book of Acts in church on the evening before the Paschal service. For the same reason, the Acts are read aloud at the daily liturgy during the entire period of the Pentecostarion.

The Book of Acts, according to its own writer (see Acts 1:1–2), is his second book written for a certain Theophilus. Thus, it is evident that the Book of Acts was written as a continuation of the third Gospel, and its author is obviously none other than the author of the third Gospel, the Apostle and evangelist Luke, who was himself a fellow laborer and fellow traveler of St Paul. The authorship of St Luke is attested as early as the second half of the second century in the *Letter of the Churches of Vienne and Lyons to the Churches of Asia and Phrygia* by St Irenaeus of Lyons, by Clement of Alexandria, and by Tertullian as well as in the ancient Muratorian Canon, in the writings of Origen, in the *Peshitta*, in the ancient Syriac translation of the Bible, and in the work of many other later Christian writers. Hints to the existence of this book, as well as direct quotations, are found in even earlier writings, such as those by St Ignatius of Antioch, St Polycarp of Smyrna, and St Justin Martyr.

We also have internal evidence for St Luke's authorship. The writer is often a direct participant in the events (even using the first person plural, instead of the third person), being a fellow traveler and fellow laborer of St Paul (see 16:10–17, 20:5–15, 21:1–17, 27:1–28). This also is why the writer speaks mostly (and in the second half, exclusively) about the apostolic work of St Paul. Even the tone of the narrative and the style of the book remind the reader of the Gospel according to St Luke.

The Time and Place of the Composition of the Book of Acts

The last events of Acts indicate that the Apostle Paul lived in Rome for two years, constantly preaching the Gospel (28:30–31). Nothing is written of his martyrdom at the hands of Emperor Nero on June 29, A.D. 67. Tradition tells us that the Apostle Paul, having been vindicated at his trial before Caesar—the trial occurred after his two-year imprisonment in Rome—returned to Jerusalem and went on a fourth missionary journey. From this, we can conclude that the Book of Acts was written by St Luke in A.D. 63 or 64 in Rome. In the Epistles to the Colossians (4:14) and Philemon (v. 24), Paul mentions that St Luke resided with him in Rome. Blessed Jerome also witnessed that the Acts were written in Rome. Only such gnostic heretics as the Marcionites, Manicheans, Ebionites, and Severian Encratites tried to impugn the authenticity of the Book of Acts, because its contents too sharply contradicted their false teachings. For this reason, they hated this book and tried to cast doubts on its authenticity.

The Content of the Book of Acts

The Book of Acts contains a summary of events beginning with the ascension of the Lord Jesus Christ and ending with St Paul's arrival in Rome. Therefore, its scope encompasses about thirty years of the Church's history. The first half of the book (chapters 1–12) concerns itself primarily with the labors of the Apostle Peter among the Jews in Palestine, while the second half (chapters 13–28) describes the Apostle Paul's preaching among the Gentiles and the spread of Christianity beyond Palestine. Thus, the Book of Acts paints a picture of the Christian Church, having been established among the Jews of Palestine according to the words of the Lord Himself (and this despite the stubborn unbelief of the greater mass of the Jewish nation), spreading into the pagan milieu, eventually reaching Asia and southern Europe. The content of the Book of Acts chapter by chapter is as follows:

Chapter 1: Prologue. The Lord's instruction and promises to the apostles before the ascension, and His ascension. The Apostle Peter's speech about the necessity of choosing a replacement for Judas Iscariot. The choosing of Matthias.

Chapter 2: The descent of the Holy Spirit on the apostles on the day of Pentecost. The Apostle Peter's speech and its powerful effect. The character of the life and religious and moral state of the first Christian community in Jerusalem.
Chapter 3: The miraculous healing by St Peter of the man lame from birth. The Apostle Peter's speech in connection with this healing, together with a call for repentance.
Chapter 4: The imprisonment of the Apostles Peter and John. Their questioning before the Sanhedrin, who forbids them to continue preaching in the name of Jesus and releases them. The prayer of the apostles and the sending of the grace of the Holy Spirit on the assembled faithful. The mutual love of the members of the first Christian community.
Chapter 5: Ananias and Sapphira, who hid part of their money from the community. Miracles accomplished by the apostles. The Sanhedrin's new persecution of the apostles, their imprisonment, their deliverance by an angel, their continued preaching in the temple and their answer before the Sanhedrin. Gamaliel's advice. The apostles are released after being beaten. They accept their beating with joy.
Chapter 6: The choosing of the seven deacons. The preaching of Archdeacon Stephen. The Sanhedrin accuses him of blasphemy against the Law of Moses.
Chapter 7: Archdeacon Stephen's words before the Sanhedrin and his martyrdom.
Chapter 8: The first great persecution of the Church in Jerusalem after the death of Stephen. The planting of the Church in Samaria by Deacon Philip. The sending down of the Holy Spirit on the Samarian believers by the Apostles Peter and John. The baptism of Simon Magus. Philip's conversion of the eunuch of the Ethiopian queen.
Chapter 9: Saul's conversion to Christ on the road to Damascus. His baptism by Ananias. Saul's preaching in Damascus. Flight from the Jews who plan to kill him. Saul's sojourn in Jerusalem. The Apostle Peter in Lydda, and Aeneas's healing. The Apostle Peter in Joppa, and the raising of Tabitha from the dead.
Chapter 10: The first Gentile, Cornelius the centurion, converted to the Lord after the Apostle Peter's vision.
Chapter 11: The Apostle Peter rebuked by the circumcised (i.e., by the Jewish Christians) for his association with the uncircumcised. Peter's explanation. Preaching Christ beyond Palestine, especially in Antioch. Barnabas and Saul in Antioch. The prophecy about the coming drought and a collection for the Christians in Judea.
Chapter 12: Herod persecutes the Church. James is martyred. Peter is imprisoned and miraculously freed by an angel after the Church's prayers. Herod's death. Barnabas and Saul return from Jerusalem to Antioch.

Chapter 13: Barnabas and Saul travel to Cyprus and convert the proconsul Sergius Paulus. Their preaching in Perga and Pisidia. The Apostle Paul's speech in the synagogue, the stubborn unbelief of the Jews, and his subsequent preaching to the Gentiles. Persecutions against Barnabas and Paul.

Chapter 14: Paul and Barnabas in Iconium, Lystra, and Derbe. Healing the lame in Lystra and the attempts of the local pagans to offer them sacrifices. Persecutions. Paul is stoned. The return to Antioch by way of the cities with the newly established Christian communities.

Chapter 15: Confusion in the Church of Antioch concerning adherence for Gentiles to the rites of the Mosaic Law. The Apostolic Council in Jerusalem. Disagreement between Paul and Barnabas. Paul and Silas begin the second missionary journey.

Chapter 16: Paul in Lystra and Derbe. The circumcision of Timothy. Journey to Troas. The vision of the Macedonian man and the journey to Macedonia. Paul in Philippi: the conversion of Lydia, the exorcism of the spirit of prophecy, the imprisonment of Paul and Silas, and their miraculous deliverance. The conversion of the prison guard.

Chapter 17: Paul and Silas preach in Thessalonica and then in Berea. Paul in Athens. His speech in the Areopagus.

Chapter 18: Paul preaches in Corinth. The Lord encourages him in a vision. Paul, accused before the proconsul Gallio, is then released and travels to Ephesus, visiting other cities along the way and encouraging his disciples. Apollos, after being instructed by Priscilla and Aquila, preaches in Achaia.

Chapter 19: The third missionary journey of Paul. His arrival in Ephesus. The baptism of John's disciples and the calling down of the Spirit on them. Paul's miracles in Ephesus and their effect. The Jewish exorcists who were beaten by evil spirit. The burning of the magical books. Riots against Paul and the Christians incited by Demetrius the silversmith.

Chapter 20: Paul's journey to Macedonia, Greece, and his return to Troas. Paul resurrects Eutychus in Troas. Further journeys to Miletus. Paul's farewell speech to the presbyters of Ephesus.

Chapter 21: The Christians try to convince Paul not to return to Jerusalem, but without success. His journey from Miletus to Caesaria. Paul in Caesaria and Agabus's prophecy concerning Paul's bonds. Paul's arrival in Jerusalem, the riots in the streets, and his imprisonment.

Chapter 22: Paul's speech to the people concerning his conversion and his calling to the dignity of apostleship. The cries of the people who wanted him flogged; the canceling of his flogging. Paul before the Sanhedrin.

Chapter 23: The high priest Ananias commands Paul be struck on the mouth. The argument between the Pharisees and Sadducees. The Lord encourages

Paul. The Jews' final decision to kill Paul. Paul sent to Felix in Caesaria under heavy guard.

Chapter 24: The Apostle Paul before the governor Felix. The Jews accuse him, and he defends himself. The postponement of judgment. Paul preaches Christ to Felix and his wife. Felix is replaced by Festus as governor; Paul remains imprisoned.

Chapter 25: Governor Festus in Jerusalem; the Jews take the advantage to complain about Paul. Judgment before Festus. Paul appeals to Caesar. King Agrippa and Bernice come to Caesaria. Paul is brought to the place of hearing before Agrippa.

Chapter 26: Paul's defense before Agrippa, Festus, and others, together with an account of the circumstances of his life and conversion. Paul is declared to be innocent.

Chapter 27: Paul is sent to Rome for judgment before Caesar. Paul's warning, which is ignored, and a storm at sea. The ship runs aground; all those on the ship are saved by swimming to shore.

Chapter 28: The hospitality of the natives on Malta. The snake whose bite did Paul no harm. Paul heals many sick on the island. Further journeys, arrival in Rome, and preaching in Rome.

The Significance of the Book of Acts

St John Chrysostom describes the importance of this book in his first homily on Acts. In this book, we see the fulfillment of those prophecies that the Lord uttered to His apostles in the Gospels. In it, we see the triumph of the faith of Christ over this fallen world, in spite of the human frailty of the apostles who had no money to ensure the success of their mission. In this book, we see how the apostles themselves became completely different people after the descent of the Holy Spirit. Fearlessly, with great self-rejection and courage, they preached the faith of Christ to the very end of the Greco-Roman civilized world, despite grievous persecutions. In a short time, they established many Christian communities who lived in the spirit of the commandments of the Gospels. The Book of Acts vividly shows us that the preaching of the Apostles was not the work of man, but of God (let us remember the words of wise Gamaliel, who counseled the Sanhedrin not to persecute the disciples of Christ in Acts 5:38–39). Most useful for us is the description of the life of the first Christians, who had "one heart and one soul" (Acts 4:32) which stood in complete opposition to the rest of the world at that time, which was drowning in selfishness and all manner of sins and vices.

The Book of Acts is important for pastors of Christ's Church because it gives a model of good order and governance of the Church, established on the foundation of conciliarity (as exemplified at the Council of the Apostles in Acts 15). This book also describes the essential responsibilities of the pastor of the Church (see the Apostle Paul's conversation with the presbyters of Ephesus in Acts 20:18–35).

Of course, the most important aspect of this book is that, like no other book, it offers a witness to the great truth of Christianity—the resurrection of Christ. The best proof of the truth of Christ's resurrection is the miracles that the apostles performed, and the Book of Acts is nothing other than, first of all, the narrative concerning the apostles' miracles.

Part I

CHAPTER 3

The Church of Christ Among the Jews

ACTS CHAPTER ONE

The prologue to the Book of Acts (1:1–3). The Lord's Instruction and Promises Before the Ascension and the Ascension Itself (1:4–11). The Apostle Peter's Speech About Choosing a New Apostle in Place of Judas. The Choosing of Matthias (1:12–26).

THE PROLOGUE (1:1–3).

In the prologue, the author addresses a certain Theophilus, at the same time referring to his "former account," in which he described everything "that Jesus began to do and teach." It is all too obvious that we are dealing with the writer of the third canonical Gospel, written by Luke for the same "Theophilus." St Luke immediately points to the organic unity between his Gospel and this second book, which should be read as a continuation of the first. Of course, when he says that he wrote of all that Jesus did, he meant it only relatively, as St John considered it impossible to depict everything that Christ did and said (see John 21:25). Here, "all" means "all that is necessary" to become better acquainted with the life, deeds, and teachings of the Lord Jesus Christ and to believe in Him as the Son of God.

Note that Luke says, "all that Jesus began both to do and teach," thereby indicating that in His earthly life, the Lord only began the work of the Gospel and will continue to do so through His apostles (whose acts are described in this book), and naturally also through their successors until the very end of the world (see Matt 28:20): "Until the day in which He was taken up." The ascension is indicated as a pivotal moment. This marked the end of the Gospel history and the beginning of apostolic history. Until this moment, the activity of the Lord on earth was visible, but from this moment His invisible work begins. "After He through the Holy Spirit had given commandments to the apostles." The importance of this pivotal moment in the history of mankind's salvation is that the Lord ascended, having left His disciples a commandment, a kind of last will and testament that expressed His final wishes concerning the spread and establishment of His teaching in the whole world. "Through the Holy Spirit," for, according to Blessed Theophylact, "wherever the Son acts, there also the Spirit is present and active, as consubstantial with the Son."[1] These commands were not given to everyone, but only to those "whom He had chosen" for a great work, "to whom He also presented Himself alive" after His Passion and death, so that the apostles could witness His resurrection to the whole world. He confirmed them in the truth of His resurrection, continuing to appear to them for forty days. Thus, the Book of Acts completes the Gospel, indicating that although the Lord no longer remained with His disciples constantly after His resurrection, He still appeared to them often and only after forty days ascended from them into heaven. During this period, He taught them the mysteries of the kingdom of God—we can assume He spoke of the establishment of this kingdom, the Church of Christ on earth, to prepare them for their upcoming apostolic work.

The Lord's Instruction and Promises Before the Ascension and the Ascension Itself (1:4–11).

"And being assembled together with them, He commanded them not to depart from Jerusalem." This required no small self-rejection on the part of the disciples, for they had no desire to stay in the city that was so antagonistic to their Master and themselves. But this was the will of God, for from Zion was the Law to come, and the word of the Lord from Jerusalem (see Isa 2:2 ff.). Where enmity against God and His Christ reached its most virulent expression, the grace of God was to be revealed in excess. From there, the preaching of the Gospel to the world would begin.

After this difficult command to remain in Jerusalem, the Lord immediately gave them a joyful promise concerning the sending of the all-powerful Protector and Guide from Almighty God—the Holy Spirit. Doubtless, Christ meant the Holy Spirit when He spoke of the "Promise of the Father," for God promised to send Him even in the Old Testament through the prophets (see Isa 44:3, Joel 3:1). "Which you have heard from Me"—Christ spoke about the Spirit many times with the apostles, especially in His final, farewell conversation, calling him "another Comforter" (Luke 12:11; Matt 10:20; John 7:12–15, 14:15–17, 26; 15:26). "For John truly baptized with water." ... even the greatest of the prophets, John the Baptist, spoke of the coming of the Holy Spirit, contrasting the water baptism that he performed with the baptism by the Holy Spirit (Matt 3:4, Luke 3:16, John 1:33). The expression "be baptized with the Holy Spirit" expresses the fullness and abundance of the gifts of the Holy Spirit. The apostles were inundated by the all-cleansing and vivifying power of the Holy Spirit. "Not many days from now." The Lord did not indicate an exact time frame for the Spirit's coming, so that expectation would encourage the apostles to constant spiritual vigilance and a joyful desire to see the fulfillment of this great promise, thereby strengthening their faith as well. This event occurred ten days after the ascension of the Lord, on the day of Jewish Pentecost, which was to become the first Christian Pentecost as well.

"Lord, will You at this time restore the kingdom to Israel?" This question shows that the Apostles still had not fully abandoned their incorrect suppositions—universal for the Jews of the time—regarding the kingdom of the Messiah. Only after the descent of the Holy Spirit were they finally reborn spiritually. They asked this question because they knew the prophecy of Joel regarding the abundant gifts of the Holy Spirit that would flow in the kingdom of the Messiah (Joel 3:1–2). The Lord wisely deflected this inappropriate question, saying, "It is not for you to know times or seasons which the Father has put in His own authority." In a few days, when the Holy Spirit would descend on them, they would no longer waste time with such questions. Their duty was to be witnesses of the Lord, that is, preachers of His Gospel, and for this, they would "receive power when the Holy Spirit has come upon you," so they could witness "in Jerusalem, and in all Judea and Samaria, and to the end of the earth." Jerusalem, the city in which the Lord was crucified, must be the first to hear the proclamation of the crucified and risen Messiah, and then the word of God must first be preached to the whole chosen nation of God in Judea, then in Samaria, as the nearest neighboring country, and only then to all the Gentiles throughout the world.

"Now when He had spoken these things, while they watched, He was taken up, and a cloud received Him out of their sight." Here, two moments are important. At first, the Lord rose up before the disciples so that they could follow him with their eyes as he ascended, soaring on the air, and then He was covered by a cloud. It is possible that this cloud was a symbol of the presence of the glory of God, as it would often appear in the Old Testament (see Matt 17:5). Astounded by the majesty of the sight, the disciples, evidently, watched for a long time, intent on the heavens where the Lord was no longer visible, until "two men" in white clothing—doubtless, angels—appeared before them. White clothing is a symbol of angelic purity and holiness; only angels can bring tidings of Christ's second coming. "Men of Galilee, why do you stand gazing up into heaven?" This question is a mild rebuke; there is no reason for them to remain so long in such inactive posture. They must prepare themselves for their coming labors, to which they have been called by the Lord.

All the thoughts of the disciples—the same can also apply to all true followers of Christ—must be directed from this time to the expectation of His glorious second coming, and their lives must be a preparation for it. "Jesus … will so come in like manner." The second coming will be like His ascension, that is, the Lord will appear again in His glorified human body and again will be visible to all mankind. That means that we cannot understand the second coming to be some kind of metaphorical or symbolic event, as some rationalists prefer to think. The Lord Himself said that He would appear "coming on the clouds of heaven with power and great glory" (Matt 24:30). The angels merely confirmed His words. Thus, the glorious second coming of the Lord will be bodily, visible, and just as obvious as His bodily resurrection.

"Then they returned to Jerusalem from the mount called Olivet." Here, we see that the Lord ascended from the Mount of Olives, which was located to the east of Jerusalem. Because Theophilus apparently did not know Palestine, St Luke explains that the Mount of Olives is a "Sabbath day's journey" from Jerusalem. According to the rabbinical teaching, one could not travel more than two thousand steps on a Sabbath. This was the distance from the farthest tents of the Jewish encampments in the desert during the time of Moses to the tabernacle. The first-century Roman Jewish historian Josephus also gives a distance from the Mount of Olives to Jerusalem, indicating that it was five or six *stadii*, the equivalent of about two-thirds of a mile. The Mount of Olives, which was the witness of the greatest indignity of Christ's life (the garden of Gethsemane is located on its western slope), now saw His greatest glorification—His ascension to the Father as the Son of God.

The Apostle Peter's Speech About Choosing a New Apostle in Place of Judas. The Choice of Matthias (1:12–26).

After returning from the Mount of Olives, all eleven of the Apostles (whom St Luke mentions explicitly by name) remained, by the Lord's command, together in the "Upper Room" of a house where they could remain in constant prayer away from the noise of the street and prepare themselves for the coming of the Spirit. It is possible that this was the same Upper Room where the Mystical Supper was held. "These all continued with one accord in prayer and supplication." These words reveal the deep religious inspiration of the disciples following the Lord's ascension. According to St Luke, they returned to Jerusalem with "great joy" (Luke 24:52). They expressed this joy in their intense common prayer. Being in Jerusalem like lambs among the wolves, they, of course, needed the extraordinary encouragement of prayer to avoid all possible temptations.

The Apostles were together "with the women and Mary the Mother of Jesus." These were the myrrh-bearing women, the witnesses to the burial and resurrection of Christ. The so-called brothers of Jesus were here as well. Only recently, they had refused to believe in Him (see John 7:5), but now they were among the faithful. Other believers also participated, making the total number about 120 people.

The Apostle Peter, "the mouth of the apostles, always fiery and chief among the apostles," as St John Chrysostom refers to him, stood up among the disciples "in those days"—that is, in the time period between the ascension and Pentecost—and offered the assembly to choose a new apostle to take the place of the apostate

Judas Iscariot. It is interesting that "Peter does everything with the common consent, and nothing on his own, nothing imperiously."[2] The Apostle Peter described the profound fall of Judas by saying it was foreordained by God. It is important to note that this foreknowledge does not destroy human free will, for the predestination of God, expressed in prophecy, is founded only on His foreknowledge. God knows how a person will use his free will, and depending on this free choice, God predestines. Lest Judas's fall become a temptation for the others, St Peter offered prophecies from the Old Testament, which made clear that this evening was nothing extraordinary, for it already had been foretold, and so it had to happen.

From St Peter's words, we find out the details of Judas's terrible death (absent in the Gospels). The phrase "this man purchased a field with the wages of iniquity," of course, is idiomatic, indicating that the money Judas received from the chief priests was later used to buy land to bury wanderers, called by the locals "Akel Dama, that is, Field of Blood." St Luke explains the word to Theophilus, who did not know Hebrew. Those listening to St Peter, of course, did not require such explication; therefore, we must not think that these are the exact words of St Peter as uttered to the assembly. The prophetic words concerning Judas are taken from the Psalms (Ps 68:26, 108:8). The first quotation is slightly different from the Psalms, whereas the latter is a direct quotation. Both of these Psalms describe a righteous man who suffers innocently at the hands of his enemies. Both of these Psalms also are filled with imprecations in the form of prayer, mostly directed at a single enemy.

Doubtless, this innocent sufferer—no matter who he was in historical fact, David himself or some other man—was the foreshadowing of the Messiah, our Lord Jesus Christ. His enemies, in turn, foreshadowed the enemies of the Lord, those who betrayed Him to be crucified. Chief among them was Judas, and this is why the Apostle Peter slightly changes the wording in the first quotation from the plural to the singular, and the imprecation against *enemies* he changes to a single *enemy*—Judas Iscariot. "Let his dwelling place be desolate": this is a symbol of the wrath of God against those living in this place. When applied to Judas, it means that his place among the apostles is now vacant. Instead of an unworthy one, the place must be filled by a worthy man, something that is also expressed in the Psalm: "let another take his office." Because the prophecy concerning Judas's expulsion from the ranks of the apostles was fulfilled, the other prophecy must come to pass as well—his place must be filled by another, reinstating the number of the Twelve, as established by the Lord Himself.

It is likely that the Lord Himself also commanded this to be done, even if we do not have such a commandment in the Gospels. The only absolute condition for choosing a new apostle was this—he must be an eyewitness to the entire life and work of Jesus Christ. This is important, because the apostles themselves were first of all eyewitnesses, as the Lord Himself called them (Luke 24:48), for they must witness before the entire world concerning what they saw and heard (Acts 4:20). This is what gives their preaching such power and conviction. In addition, the fact of the new apostle's constant abiding with the Lord for the three and a half years was proof enough of his faith, love, and loyalty to the Lord. Such a person could safely be entrusted with the labors of the apostolic ministry.

"Beginning from the baptism of John to that day when He was taken up from us." Here, Peter indicated the beginning and the end of Christ's earthly ministry, all of which the new apostle must have seen with his own eyes. "One of these must become a witness with us of His resurrection." This is the second important condition for choosing a new apostle, because the testimony to the reality of Christ's resurrection is the most important aspect of the apostolic ministry, because the resurrection is the foundational truth of Christianity. It was absolutely necessary for the new apostle to be an eyewitness to the resurrection of the crucified Messiah.

Two men satisfied all the conditions: "Joseph called Barsabas, who was surnamed Justus, and Matthias." These men do not appear in the Gospel narrative. Some have suggested that they were in the number of the seventy apostles. The final choice from these two was left to the Lord Himself through the casting of lots and intense prayer, asking God to reveal His choice. Thus, there was a dual action in this choosing—human and divine. The apostles and the assembled faithful chose two men, and the Lord, by their prayers, indicated His choice. "O Lord, who knowest the hearts of all." This is how they prayed to the Lord. The Lord is a knower of hearts, knowing the soul of every person, and He knew which of these two would be more capable of bearing the heavy burden of apostleship. Choosing by lot was an Old Testament institution, and the casting of lots was seen as the direct action of God Himself (see Lev 16:8; Num 17:1, 34:13, Josh 14:2; 1 Kgdms 10:20). Usually names were written on pieces of paper, which then were placed in a vessel, shaken up, and whatever name was pulled out was considered to be the chosen one. "And the lot fell on Matthias." This was seen to be the will of God, and "he was numbered with the eleven apostles."

St Matthias later preached in Judea and Ethiopia and was stoned in Jerusalem by the order of the chief priest Ananias, who had a special hatred for Christians. The Holy Apostle Matthias was commemorated by the Orthodox Church on August 9. The second candidate, Joseph Justus, later became the bishop of Eleutheropolis and also died a martyr's death. The Orthodox Church celebrates his memory on October 30.

Acts Chapter Two

The Descent of the Holy Spirit on the Apostles on Pentecost and the Confusion of the People (2:1–13). The Apostle Peter's Speech and Its Effect on the Listeners (2:14–41). The Religious and Moral State of the First Christian Community in Jerusalem (2:42–47).

THE DESCENT OF THE HOLY SPIRIT ON THE APOSTLES ON PENTECOST AND THE CONFUSION OF THE PEOPLE (2:1–13).

The great event of the descent of the Holy Spirit on the apostles is called by some the "birthday of the Church of Christ." At the same time, this event was also a conclusion of the entire work of God's economy of salvation. According to St Theophan the Recluse, "what God the Father willed to be and what the Son of God accomplished in Himself, that the Holy Spirit came today to give to the faithful."[3] Illumined by the Holy Spirit, the apostles fearlessly began to preach Christ crucified and risen. The Church of Christ began to grow and spread at first among the Jews of Palestine, then eventually among the Gentiles in the whole world, and even "to the end of the earth" (Acts 1:8).

This occurred "when the Day of Pentecost had fully come," the high point of the Jewish feast of Pentecost. The Law of Moses decreed to celebrate solemnly the fiftieth day after the day following the Sabbath of the Passover, counting seven full weeks from that day (Lev 23:15). The Jewish Passover in the year of Christ's death occurred on Friday evening. The first day of Passover was thus the Sabbath, and the morning after the Sabbath was the Sunday of Christ's resurrection. From that day, seven weeks must be counted. Thus, in that year, the celebration of the Jewish Pentecost occurred on a Sunday (and therefore Christian Pentecost always falls on a Sunday). The Pentecost of the Jews was established to bless the harvest or the first fruits, because the first harvest of seeds planted immediately after Passover brought fruit roughly at this time. This feast also was combined with the remembrance of the giving of the Law on Mt Sinai. This was one of the three major "pilgrim" feasts of the Jewish calendar (Passover, Pentecost, Booths), on which all Jewish men were obligated to travel as pilgrims to Jerusalem for the celebration.

The concurrence of the descent of the Holy Spirit with Jewish Pentecost, of course, is no coincidence. In fact, it is symbolic. By this time, the apostles had matured and blossomed spiritually, and so this was the time when the fullness of the gifts of the Spirit descended on them, and thus they themselves became the first fruits of Christ's work of redemption. In addition to the apostles, the first fruits of this work were the three thousand people who were baptized on that day. Just as the Christian Pascha replaced the Jewish Passover, so too did the Christian Pentecost replace the Jewish Pentecost. As Blessed Theophylact of Ochrid noted in his commentary,

> It was appropriate for the grace of the Spirit to be given on the same day as the giving of the ancient Law, because as the Saviour willed to commit Himself to His passion in no other time than the time of the killing of the lamb, in order to tie the truth with the prefiguration. Thus also the coming of the Spirit could not have been given at any other time than the day when the Law was given, in order to show that the Holy Spirit is the same Lawgiver of both the Old and the New Covenants.... In the same

> way that on Pentecost sheaves of the new fruits were gathered by many people from many different places to Jerusalem, so on this day it was appropriate that the first fruits of all nations living under heaven should gather into a single sheaf of piety, brought to God through the apostolic preaching.[4]

"They were all with one accord in one place." The account in Acts makes it obvious that not only the Twelve were present, but also all the faithful, perhaps even more than those 120 mentioned in the first chapter. In verse 14, the Twelve are clearly differentiated from the other participants of this great event. This gathering, we can assume, occurred in the same Upper Room where the disciples probably met every day after the Mystical Supper. "And suddenly there came a sound from heaven, as of a rushing mighty wind, and it filled the whole house where they were sitting." They were awaiting the coming of the Holy Spirit, but of course they did not know when exactly this promise would be fulfilled. Neither did they know the manner of this coming, and so St Luke calls the descent "sudden," unexpected for them, especially because this was the hour of morning prayer, and most likely they were just getting ready to go to the temple to pray. The sound "as of a rushing wind" obviously was not an actual physical wind, but only the sound of it. This sound came down from above, filling the whole house, and it was so strong that it attracted the attention of many people who had gathered for the feast in Jerusalem.

"Then there appeared to them divided tongues, as of fire, and one sat upon each of them." The tongues only appeared to be fire, but they were not fire, just as the sound appeared to be wind, but it was not wind. The noise was the audible sign of the descent of the Holy Spirit, and the tongues were the visible sign. The sound of wind was a symbol of the mighty power that the Holy Spirit gave to the apostles and to all the faithful, while the tongues of fire were a symbol that all had received the gift of fiery speech that could burn away all impurity and falsehood, everything contrary to the truth, like fire.[5]

Immediately after these external signs came the inner revelation: "and they were all filled with the Holy Spirit and began to speak with other tongues, as the Spirit gave them utterance." Even before this moment, the apostles were given some spiritual gifts, but now they were filled with the Holy Spirit, for the fullness of gracious spiritual gifts now had descended upon them. They were transfigured, purified, sanctified, and enlightened by the action of the Spirit of God. It was as if they became completely different, new people, with the Holy Spirit as their constant inspiration and guide. The external manifestation of this grace-filled transfiguration was the speaking in tongues, something that Christ Himself foretold (Mark 16:17). As soon as this divine fire lit their souls, they began to praise and thank God in the natural exuberance of their holy ecstasy, glorifying the majesty of God.

This gratitude to God was expressed aloud in various tongues, which attracted even more attention from the masses of people who had come to Jerusalem for the feast from various countries, both near and far. St Luke purposely lists all the countries to show how many different tongues were spoken by the disciples of Christ after the descent of the Spirit. Here were inhabitants of eastern and western Asia, Africa, and Europe, and they all heard their native tongues. This was also symbolic. We see the foreshadowing of the Church of Christ, into which all nations and races would enter, so that with one mind and heart all would praise God.

The gift of tongues is understandable: it was necessary to spread the faith all over the earth. At the same time, one cannot help but remember how this same gift was once used by God as a punishment for human pride. There was once a time when "the whole earth had one language and one speech" (Gen 11:1). But man, in his pride, undertook a mad venture that God punished by sending down multiple tongues, which forced the workers to leave the work and go to different places. Now the multiplication of tongues has become a means by which diverse nations are united into a one single Church of Christ. This is beautifully expressed in the *kontakion* of Pentecost: "When the Most High came down and confused the tongues, He divided the nations, but when He distributed the tongues of fire, He called all to unity. And with one accord we glorify the All-Holy Spirit."[6]

"And there were dwelling in Jerusalem Jews, devout men, from every nation under heaven." Here St Luke speaks both of the Jews who previously lived in other countries and then moved to Jerusalem for religious reasons and the pilgrims who assembled for the feast, and thus were in the city for a short time. About the time of Christ's earthly life, the Jewish diaspora was extensive. Some of the Jews abandoned Palestine unwillingly, as military captives, but some went into diaspora voluntarily, often for reasons of trade and business.

"And when this sound occurred, the multitude came together, and were confused, because everyone heard them speak in his own language." Apparently the sound of wind rushing into the house where the disciples were assembled could be heard at a considerable distance, and it was so clear that the listeners could pinpoint the exact house. The strangeness of such a phenomenon attracted a huge crowd to the house—it is possible these people were on their way to the temple to pray. Probably, a wide courtyard was in front of the house. The people were amazed at the inexplicable phenomenon: the apostles—who by their clothing showed their Galilean provenance (i.e., their lack of education)—were speaking in various tongues, so that every person in the crowd could hear his own tongue or dialect. Galilee was known as a country of the unlearned folk, not particularly known for their education, and so the gathered people were amazed that Galileans could speak so many different languages and dialects. We can assume that the apostles, glorifying God in different languages, had come out onto the flat roof of the house, and the people listened to them from the courtyard of the house, surrounding the house and filling the square completely.

"So they were all amazed and perplexed, saying to one another, 'Whatever could this mean?' Others mocking said, 'They are full of new wine.'" Evidently, not everyone reacted in the same way to this event. Pious people saw it as something miraculous and tried to find out what it could mean. But frivolous and unbelieving people, perhaps belonging to the sects opposed to Christ the Saviour, the Pharisees and the Sadducees, began to interpret this event with the crudest of explanations—by the effect of wine, essentially insulting the Spirit of God. In the same way, unbelief, anger, and frivolousness always try to give the most exalted phenomena of the spiritual life the crudest of explanations, being unable to understand that which is spiritual (see 1 Cor 2:14–15).

The Apostle Peter's Speech and Its Effect on the Listeners (2:14–41). The amazement of some, and the crude mockery of others, inspired the apostles to explain the miracle to the people. The gift of tongues was given to all the disciples of Christ who were in the house, but now only the Twelve came forth, and in their name the Apostle Peter addresses the people with the first apostolic proclamation. He "raised his voice"—his speech was full of boldness, it was triumphant, vivid, and instructive. St Peter spoke to the people as though they represented all of Jerusalem. Gently and meekly he removed any suspicion of drunkenness, "for these are not drunk, as you suppose, since it is only the third hour of the day." This was the time of the morning prayer (around 9 A.M.), before which no Jewish person would even eat, especially on such a great feast as Pentecost.

In his explanation, Peter referenced the prophecy of Joel (3:1–3), spoken over eight hundred years before. In this prophecy, the Lord, through the mouth of the prophet, gave a promise to His people that the gifts of the Spirit would be poured down on all believing people, and together with the promise of salvation for the righteous, He warned of judgment for the unrighteous. The first words of the prophecy—"After this"—Peter replaced with the new introductory words, "and it shall come to pass in the last days," a prophetic expression that refers to the end of the time of the Old Covenant and the beginning of the New. This replacing of the indeterminate "after this" made it clear that Peter considered it impossible that Joel's prophecy could have referred to any event in the times of the Old Testament, but instead believed it to have been fulfilled now, in the New Testament time.

"I will pour out of My Spirit on all flesh," instead of the original words of the prophet, "I will pour out My Spirit," communicated the same meaning, but the apostle indicated that these gifts of the Holy Spirit are shared out among each one of the faithful individually. This "pouring out" is an image of the abundance of these gifts of the Holy Spirit, like rain or water pouring out of a vessel. The pouring out "on all flesh" indicates that all mankind will receive these gifts. This, of course, refers to all those who enters into the newly initiated kingdom of the Messiah (see Isa 40:5, 66:24), for only the members of the Christ's kingdom will receive this grace of the Holy Spirit. Before the coming of Christ, the greater part of mankind, the Gentiles, were deprived completely of the gifts of the Holy Spirit, while grace was given to some of the Jews who were chosen for a special ministry. In Christianity, every one of the faithful receives these gifts of grace through the sacraments. The fulfillment of this prophecy began on the day of Pentecost.

As examples, the prophecy indicates certain manifestations of these gifts of the Holy Spirit that already were known in the Old Testament: prophecies, visions, dreams, and other means of divine revelation. "Your sons and your daughters ... your young men ... your old men"—this indicates that the Holy Spirit will pour His gifts on all, with no distinction of age or gender. The phrase "and on My menservants and on My maidservants I will pour out My Spirit in those days" is interesting, because in the Old Testament, we know of no instances of slaves receiving the gifts of the Holy Spirit or of slaves becoming prophets. In the New Testament, however, the bonds of slavery will be destroyed and the Holy Spirit will pour out His gifts on all, regardless of their social status, for in the kingdom of Christ, all are equal before the Lord, for all are His servants.

This foretelling of the abundant pouring out of the Holy Spirit is connected to a prophecy concerning the judgment of the impious world, and the salvation of the true worshippers of the true God. The signs of this coming Last Judgment of God over mankind are "blood and fire and vapor of smoke." These are the symbols of bloodshed, rioting, wars, and desolation. Together with these signs will come heavenly signs, including eclipses of the sun and the moon. These terrors, in the literary style of the Scriptures, indicate the calamities in the world of man that will be the harbingers of God's judgment over the world. All this will occur "before the coming of the great and awesome day of the Lord." In the Old Testament, this day was understood to be the "day of the Messiah," that is, the beginning of his glorious reign, but in the New Testament, this is seen to be the day of the Messiah's judgment over the world, the day of the Final Judgment.

However, "whoever calls on the name of the Lord shall be saved" from this judgment. Of course, this person is not the one who calls on the Lord only after His second coming, or only with his lips. As St John Chrysostom explains, "It is not enough to call on Him, for Christ Himself said that not everyone who says to Me, 'Lord, Lord,' will enter the kingdom of heaven, but only the one who says it with inward earnest affection, with a life more than commonly good, with the confidence which is meet."[7]

Of course, here the Scriptures mean the righteous men from among those who truly believe in the Lord.

How is this prophecy of Joel related to the events of Pentecost?

When the apostle explained to his listeners that the miraculous event that they witnessed is the fulfillment of the prophecy of Joel, this explanation immediately gave rise to the thought that the time of the Messiah had already come. But where is He? Who is He? And so, in his subsequent speech, Peter began to preach the good news concerning Christ. He told his listeners that the Messiah already had appeared as "Jesus of Nazareth, a Man attested by God to you by miracles, wonders, and signs."

Everyone knew of Christ's miracles, and Peter reminded his listeners of them as true proofs of His messianic dignity. For the Jews of that time, however, the Cross that He carried was a great temptation and stumbling block. To remove this temptation, Peter added that the betrayal and death of Christ occurred "by the determined purpose and foreknowledge of God." Removing their doubts that God could be crucified and die, and to be better understood by his listeners from among the Jews, the holy apostle spoke of Christ as a Man, the Son of David. Therefore, he said, "God raised [Him] up," even though Christ, as the Son of God, rose from the dead by His own power and authority (see John 10:18).

Speaking of the resurrection of the Lord, St Peter offers convincing proof from the Psalms of David (Ps 15:8–11). The Psalmist described a righteous man who had close communion with God and who expressed joy that this communion would not end with death, that his soul would not remain in hell, that even his body would not become corrupt, but that he would continue to enjoy fullness of life in God and joy in communion with Him. The apostle directly indicated that David could not be speaking of himself, since David "is both dead and buried." Therefore, David must have been speaking of the Messiah. David said this, "being a prophet," knowing the future as God revealed it to him, and "knowing that God had sworn with an oath to him that of the fruit of his body, according to the flesh, He would raise up the Christ to sit on his throne." This we indeed find in the Second Book of Kingdoms 7:12–16, in which God promised David that his house would not fall and the throne of his kingdom would be eternal. This promise, of course, could be accomplished only by the Messiah, who was to appear from the seed of David. David himself understood the promise to be such, and he glorified God in verses 18–29. Psalm 131 speaks of the same promise of God to David—that the Messiah will be his descendant, and this promise is even called an oath: "The Lord hath made a faithful oath unto David, and He shall not shrink from it" (Ps 131:11) in the sense that what is prophesied shall not ever change.

"He, foreseeing this, spoke concerning the resurrection of the Christ," continued Peter. What David said in Psalm 15:10 was accomplished not in himself, but in his descendant according to the flesh who is Jesus Christ. For Christ, having died in the flesh, descended into hell with his soul, but did not remain there. Having preached to the spirits in hell concerning His redemption of all mankind, He once again gave life to his flesh, which did not "see corruption" (see also 1 Pet 3:18–19). Peter attests to the reality of the resurrection of "this Jesus" by appealing to the witness of all of the faithful: "of which we are all witnesses."

Then, St Peter witnessed also to the ascension of Christ, which resulted in the pouring out of the grace of the Holy Spirit on the faithful. As St Peter confirmed the truth of the resurrection on the basis of the prophecies of David, so he also confirmed the truth of the ascension on the basis of a Psalm (109:1). Obviously, David did not himself ascend into heaven, but he said that God placed his Lord on His right hand. It is clear that David speaks not of himself, but of another person—the Messiah, Who is Jesus from Nazareth, Who ascended into the heavens. The Lord Jesus Christ during His earthly life applied this same prophecy to Himself (see Matt 22:42–45), and St Peter applied it specifically to the ascension of the Lord and His session at the right hand of the Father.

"Therefore let all the house of Israel know assuredly that God has made this Jesus, whom you crucified, both Lord and Christ." Jesus, crucified by them, is the same Messiah of whom the prophets spoke. "Whom you crucified": this is a bold and powerful statement, through which the apostle wanted to pierce the hearts of his listeners as with a sharp knife. God raised and glorified this Jesus, but you crucified Him! "He does well to end with this," said St John Chrysostom, "thereby agitating their minds."[8]

The speech of the Holy Apostle Peter truly had a powerful effect on the listeners. "They were cut to the heart," coming to a state of true compunction, seeing how grievously they had sinned before God and His Messiah. The divinely inspired words of St Peter, confirmed by the miracle they had witnessed with their own eyes, firmly convinced them of the Messianic dignity of Jesus of Nazareth, and they turned to Peter and the rest of the Twelve with a question full of respect, love, and trust: "Men and brethren, what shall we do?" That is, how shall we wipe away our transgression? How shall we receive forgiveness for our sins and enter into communion with the Messiah that we rejected?

Peter, on behalf of all the apostles, points to the path of reconciliation with God that lies not in the external rites of Old Testament piety, but in repentance and baptism. "Repent, and let every one of you be baptized in the name of Jesus Christ for the remission of sins; and you shall receive the gift of the Holy Spirit." Here the apostle demands from the Jews the same condition for entry into the kingdom of the Messiah that St John the Baptist and Christ Himself required (see Matt 3:2, 4:17). The first and most essential condition for entry is repentance, that is, the firm resolution to change one's life at its very root. In particular, for the Jews, that meant a rejection of Judaism and conversion to Christianity.

The second condition is baptism in the name of Jesus Christ. These words do not contradict the command of the Lord Himself to baptize "in the name of the Father, and of the Son, and of the Holy Spirit." They indicate only the most important aspect of the faith and confession of those who are baptized—that is, they must believe in Christ as the Messiah and with this faith approach the baptismal font.

In return for the fulfillment of these two conditions, the apostle promised them two rewards: forgiveness of sins and the gifts of the Holy Spirit. The salvation of man is accomplished by this twofold path: by the laying aside of the old man with his sinful deeds and by the putting on of the new man, which is the "new creation" of mankind by the power of the grace of the Holy Spirit.

"For the promise is to you and to your children, and to all who are afar off, as many as the Lord our God will call." This promise of God, given through the prophet Joel, about the pouring out of the Holy Spirit belongs first of all to the Jews as to the chosen nation of God, and then to all the nations of the earth, that is, the Gentiles, whom the Lord also calls into His kingdom. The idea of this second calling is still not explicit in Peter's words, however, for he calls the Gentiles as those "afar off," in order not to tempt the Jews, because they believed only themselves to be worthy of the kingdom of the Messiah.

"And with many other words ..." St Luke, the writer of the Acts, does not record for us everything that Peter said to his listeners, but rather only gives the essence of all that he said in a single phrase: "be saved from this perverse generation." That is, strive to avoid that condemnation that awaits the recalcitrant Jews who stubbornly refused to believe in Christ the Messiah. The promised judgment over this perverse generation occurred quite soon afterward, in A.D. 70, when the Romans destroyed Jerusalem. The Jews who converted to Christianity avoided the horrors of this terrible divine punishment of the perverse generation. They, remembering Christ's teaching (Matt 24:15–16), fled Jerusalem with time to spare.

Of course, St Peter's words also apply to all generations of all eras, because the faithful always must strive to be saved from this world that lies in sin through faith in Christ and a life of virtue. Thus, they will avoid the punishment of God that awaits the sinful world at the Last Judgment.

The effect of these events—the pouring out of the Holy Spirit on the apostles and the speech of St Peter—was magnificent. The original small community of Christians was increased by "about three thousand souls" who accepted baptism.

The Religious and Moral State of the First Christian Community in Jerusalem (2:42–47).

All those who were newly baptized "continued steadfastly in the apostles' doctrine and fellowship, in the breaking of bread, and in prayers." All that was required of those approaching baptism was heartfelt faith in Christ and repentance; only later, gradually did the apostles instruct the new Christians in the principles of the new faith. All who believed were like a big, loving family: this brotherly union is what St Luke means by the word "fellowship." "Breaking bread" usually refers to any partaking of food, but in the Book of Acts, it has a more exalted meaning: the mystery of the Eucharist, the partaking of the Body and Blood of Christ.

In the Apostolic Church, the Eucharist was sometimes celebrated in the evening (see Acts 20:7, 11), and it often was accompanied by a meal, called the "agape meal," that is, the "love feast" (see Jude 12, 1 Cor 11:20–34). The prayers here mentioned are not the prayers in the Jerusalem Temple, which are discussed further in this chapter, but proper Christian prayers performed in homes. Thus, in these gatherings of Christians in private homes, we see the beginning of Christian worship, which at that time consisted of the instruction by the apostles, the sacrament of the Eucharist, and common prayers. Singing is not explicitly mentioned here, but because singing was typical both for worship in the temple and in the synagogue, doubtless this custom also was appropriated by the assemblies of the first Christian community.

"Then fear came upon every soul." These words indicate the impression that followed the events of Pentecost, especially the conversion of so many people to Christ at one time. The souls of the unbelievers also were filled with fear, because they could not miss seeing the hand of God in all that occurred. This sense of fear increased even more because "many wonders and signs were done through the apostles."

"Now all who believed were together, and had all things in common." The mutual love of the community so united all those who believed in Christ that they "were together," that is, they related and interacted with each other like a loving family. This kind of relationship naturally led to the mutual sharing of property. This sharing was not imposed by force, as we saw it under Communism, but was done totally voluntarily, solely on the basis of brotherly love and compassion toward those who were poor and needy. This was not a rejection of private property, because those who had possessions freely shared them with those who did not have them. They "sold their possessions and goods, and divided them among all, as anyone had need." In other words, they sold their property and their personal assets and shared with the poor, or they lay all the money at the feet of the apostles for distribution to the community. It is unclear how long the Jerusalem community disposed of their property in this way, because this communal life does not last long into the historical record. Probably, it was not a long time, for as the Christian community grew, it became more difficult to manage such an arrangement.

In other communities established by the apostles, we do not see such an arrangement. In their writings, the apostles only encouraged the Christians to be generous with alms and to practice mutual brotherly love, but they never insisted on the sharing of goods. Only from time to time did they organize collections for poorer churches, which were then given to the apostles (see Acts 11:29–30, 1 Cor 16:1).

"So continuing daily with one accord in the temple ..." Every day, the Christian community participated in worship at the Temple of Jerusalem. Christianity was not a sect within Judaism, but rather, it was the completion and fulfillment of true Judaism. The entirety of the temple worship was established on the expectation of the Messiah, and so Christians could freely worship in the Second Temple. Because the Christians believed in a Messiah Who had already come, their own unique worship would need time to develop in a form distinct from the worship of the Old Testament Judaism.

The beginning of such unique Christian worship was the establishment of the sacrament of the Eucharist, which in Acts is called the "breaking of bread." To celebrate this mystery, the first Christians gathered in private homes—"from house to house"—where the Eucharist would be served in conjunction with the evening agape meal. The general character of these Christian gatherings is characterized by these words: "with gladness and simplicity of heart." This is the fruit of living faith and the purity of a heart deeply involved in a burgeoning spiritual life, illumined by the abundant gifts of the Holy Spirit.

Because of this, Christians were a model of true piety, even for the rest of the Jews who did not believe in Christ. Therefore, many respected them as "having favor with all the people." This favorable reputation of Christians was the reason for the gradual increase in converts, an event that St Luke ascribes to the work of the Lord Himself: "and the Lord added to the church daily those who were being saved."

Acts Chapter Three

The Miraculous Healing of the Man Lame from Birth (3:1–11). Peter's Sermon and His Call to Repentance (3:12–26).

The Miraculous Healing of the Man Lame from Birth (3:1–11).

After the general characterization of the life of the first Christian community in Jerusalem, the writer of the Acts begins an account of specific events, beginning with miraculous healing of a man lame from birth, which led to the second mass conversion to Christ.

St Luke does not indicate when this miracle occurred, but we can assume that some time had passed after Pentecost, as immediately after the second mass conversion, St Luke gives another general characterization of the community's life, not much different from the first, and there would have been no reason to give it had the miracle taken place soon after Pentecost.

"Now Peter and John went up together to the temple at the hour of prayer, the ninth hour." As we have seen, the Temple of Jerusalem continued to be a holy place of prayer for all Christians, including the apostles. By the time of Christ's earthly life, three times were established for a public daily prayer: at the third, sixth, and ninth hour (which roughly corresponds to our 9 A.M., 12 P.M., and 3 P.M.). The third and ninth hours coincided with the time of morning and evening sacrifices, as mandated by the Law. Traces of this tripartite prayer structure are seen even in ancient Jewish history. In Babylon, the prophet Daniel prayed on his knees three times a day (Dan 6:10), and one of David's psalms indicates that prayer must be performed in the evening, morning, and at noonday (Ps 54:18).

"And a certain man lame from his mother's womb was carried, whom they laid daily at the gate of the temple …" This man was already over forty (see Acts 4:22), which makes this miracle especially amazing. The Lord once healed a man blind from birth, and St Peter now heals a man lame from birth. This is the fulfillment of the Lord's promise that those who believe in Him will do the same works that He did Himself (John 14:12). The lame man sat at the gate "called Beautiful." Most likely, this gate was the central, eastern gate leading to the court of the Gentiles, which Josephus described as the most beautiful gate of the temple.[9] As is the universal custom in all times, the poor man begged alms of those entering the temple to pray. When the Apostles Peter and John walked past him, he directed his usual request to them as well.

"And fixing his eyes on him, with John, Peter said, 'Look at us.'" It is interesting how the apostles and the lame man lock gazes here; it is as if they are both preparing for the miracle. The apostles looked at the poor man with eyes full of Christian love and compassion, and they wanted to gauge the poor man's level of spiritual receptivity by his eyes. Also, they wanted him to gather himself, so to speak, to inspire faith and hope within him. As in other such cases, Peter spoke as a representative of all the apostles: "Silver and gold I do not have, but what I do have I give you: In the name of Jesus Christ of Nazareth, rise up and walk."

With these words, the apostle destroyed the poor man's hope of receiving any money, but he inspired hope in another gift—a greater gift than this poor man could ever have expected. It is interesting that Peter spoke with full conviction of his ability to accomplish the miracle. This conviction was doubtless founded on those promises that the Lord Himself made to the apostles (Mark 16:18, Luke 9:1, John 14:12), as well as a sense within himself of the incredible power of the Holy Spirit, something that Peter hints at in his words "what I do have."

"In the name of Jesus Christ of Nazareth, rise up and walk." The apostle accomplished the miracle by the name of Christ, confirming vividly that Jesus who was crucified and died, is alive, and that He is the source of healing for all men. To inspire even greater faith in the lame man, St Peter took him by the hand and raised him up. The healed man did not go home, but immediately entered the temple to thank God for his healing. All the people, already gathered for the appointed time of prayer, having recognized the well-known lame man, were filled with fear and wonder. The healed man, full of gratitude, did not leave the side of his healers, Peter and John, loudly glorifying God and, evidently, the apostles as well. Of course, this attracted everyone's attention. They were at this point in a large covered gallery that followed the Beautiful Gate, called Solomon's Porch. According to Josephus, this area was the only part of the original Solomon's Temple to survive its destruction by Nebuchadnezzar in 587 B.C., which is why it was named after Solomon after the temple's restoration.

Peter's Sermon and His Call to Repentance (3:12–26).

Taking advantage of the huge crowd and the people's amazement at the miracle, the Apostle Peter turned to them to preach. This sermon can be divided into two parts. In the first, St Peter indicated the true Source of healing and the purpose of the miracle, explaining that it was God, not the apostles, who performed the miracle to glorify the Lord Jesus, Who had been rejected and killed by Israel. In the second part, he encouraged the people to repent and turn to Christ to receive forgiveness of sins and to become participants in the messianic blessings, promised by the prophets. In this sermon, as in St Peter's first speech on Pentecost, he focused on the witness of the Old Testament to Christ's messianic dignity.

"Men of Israel, why do you marvel at this?" The apostle even seems to be rebuking the people for their amazement. This is because the people, perhaps, looked at the apostles as men endowed with some sort of magical power or as those who attained some special level of piety. St Peter rejects both these possibilities and instead emphasizes that the miracle was not performed by their own power, but it was only Christ who worked through them. Just as the Lord Himself ascribed all His works to His heavenly Father, so the apostles now attributed these works to the Lord Jesus Christ and to His Father.

"The God of Abraham, Isaac, and Jacob, the God of our fathers, glorified His Servant Jesus, whom you delivered up and denied in the presence of Pilate." This is the true source of the miracle: God glorified Jesus Christ, Whom you betrayed. The apostle purposely underlined their fault, to call them to repentance. "You denied the Holy One and the Just, and asked for a murderer to be granted to you," that is, the robber Barabbas, "and killed the Prince of life," that is, the Lord Jesus Christ, "Whom God raised from the dead, of which we are witnesses." God raised Jesus from the dead and now glorified Him by the healing of this lame man performed in Jesus's Name. "Through faith in His name": it was the faith in the Name of the Lord Jesus that was the power that gave healing to the lame man.

This expression can be interpreted in three different ways: (1) the healing occurred because of the faith of the apostles, (2) the healing occurred to bring the eyewitnesses of the miracle to faith in Christ, or (3) the calling of the Name of Jesus healed the lame man for the sake of his faith. Having accused his listeners of killing the Messiah, St Peter, desiring to turn them to repentance, lessened the weight of their guilt, admitting that their part in the death of Jesus was a sin of ignorance: "I know that you did it in ignorance." At the same time, the apostle points out that this deed was predetermined by the counsel and foreknowledge of God (see Acts 2:23).

"Doubtless," said St John Chrysostom, "it would have roused their opposition, had he gone off into accusation."[10] By softening his words, he showed them the possibility of forgiveness through repentance: "repent therefore and be converted, that your sins may be blotted out, so that times of refreshing may come from the presence of the Lord." This time of refreshing is the coming of the kingdom of the Messiah that the prophets foretold. "And that He may send Jesus Christ, Who was preached to you before": St Peter spoke about the second coming of Christ after the end of the world. "Whom heaven must receive": this expression means that the Lord Jesus Christ must remain with His glorified flesh in heaven from the time of ascension until His second coming, which is also called "the time of restoration of all things," *apokatastasis* in Greek, which means "restoration," in the sense of restoring a right and genuine relationship between two previously sundered parties. In other words, St Peter referred to the fact that the Jews, who had rejected their Messiah and who consequently had torn apart the covenant between them and God, will at the end of time be converted to faith in Christ, as St Paul also prophetically contemplated in Romans 11, and "God will have mercy on His people," as the prophets repeatedly foretold.

Encouraging the Jews to repent, St Peter reminded them of the especially powerful prophecy of Moses: "The Lord your God will raise up for you a Prophet … Him you shall hear." (Deut 18:15). All ancient authors, Jewish and Christian alike, considered this prophecy to refer to the Messiah. "You are the sons of the prophets, and of the covenant which God made with your fathers." To you, therefore, belong all these promises concerning the messianic kingdom and the fulfillment of the prophesies concerning Him.

Then, St Peter brought the strongest and most powerful reason for repentance: "in your seed all the families of the earth shall be blessed." This promise of God to Abraham (Gen 12:3, 18:18) must come to pass: the Messiah was not intended to be given for the Jews alone, but for all the nations of the earth. It was to the Jews "first" that God sent His Servant Jesus, and in this lies a new motivation for their repentance.

In this entire speech, St Peter, as in his first sermon, labored to show his listeners that the Christianity that he preached did not contradict the Old Testament Law in any way, but rather was its continuation and a fitting fulfillment. Once again Peter's gentleness and love for the enemies of Jesus are remarkable. He presents to them the undiluted truth, but calmly, without irritation, without bitterness, urging them to contrition over their sin and to repentance.

Acts Chapter Four

The Imprisonment of the Apostles Peter and John, and the Consequences of Peter's Sermon: Five Thousand Are Converted to Christ (4:1–4). Questioning by the Sanhedrin, Prohibition to Preach in the Name of Jesus. The Apostles Are Released (4:5–22). The Prayer of the Apostles, and the Pouring out of the Holy Spirit on the Faithful (4:23–31). The Mutual Love of the Members of the First Christian Community (4:32–37).

The Imprisonment of the Apostles Peter and John, and the Consequences of Peter's Sermon: Five Thousand Are Converted to Christ (4:1–4).

Irritated by the preaching of St Peter, the priests, Sadducees, and leaders of the temple guard seized the apostles and imprisoned them until the morning, for it was already the evening. The priests were upset that the apostles instructed the people in the temple without having any lawful authority to do so. The guards were upset that the large crowd of people was disrupting the order of the services, and the Sadducees were upset that St Peter was teaching about the resurrection from the dead, which they rejected. They interrupted Peter's sermon and "laid hands on them," of course, with the permission of the Sanhedrin.

Because it was already late and there was no time to call a session of the Sanhedrin to judge the apostles, they were imprisoned "until the next day." While the representatives of the Jewish authority treated the apostles as their enemies, the simple people were so inspired by the Apostle Peter's sermon that "about five thousand" people were converted. They believed, St Luke stresses, not because of the miracle, but because of Peter's address. They probably were prepared by everything that the apostles had been doing from the day of Pentecost and likely were impressed by the unique way of life of the first Christians, which inspired universal respect and love.

Questioning by the Sanhedrin, Prohibition to Preach in the Name of Jesus. The Apostles Are Released (4:5–22).

On the next day, the meeting of the Sanhedrin took place. This was obviously a formal and full session of the Sanhedrin, as this judgment over the apostles was considered very important. Among them was the retired High Priest Annas as well as Caiaphas, who had condemned Jesus Christ to death. Also present were the heretofore-unknown (in the Gospel narrative) John and Alexander, members of the high priest's family, who most likely had significant authority in the Sanhedrin at the time, being related to the high priest. Having placed the accused "in the midst," as was customary (see John 8:3), they asked, "By what power or by what name have you done this?"

The members of the Sanhedrin, of course, knew that the apostles performed the miracle by the Name of Jesus Christ, but they wanted the apostles to incriminate themselves in heresy, blasphemy, or even seditious intentions, or perhaps they hoped that the apostles would simply recant in fear.

"Then Peter, filled with the Holy Spirit, said to them …" He was filled with the Holy Spirit to defend the just cause, as Jesus Christ promised to His disciples before (see Matt 10:19–20). St Peter answered the question with unique power, directness, and boldness. Still giving respect to the lawful authority—even though it was unworthy—he began with the reverential address to the "rulers of the people and elders of Israel." His subsequent word choice—"If we this day are judged for a good deed done to a helpless man"—trenchantly and unmistakably demonstrated the unfairness of the judgment to which the apostles were subjected. Indeed, they showed mercy to an unfortunate person: was this a reason to bring them before a tribunal? At the same time, the apostle triumphantly and boldly witnessed before them all that the miracle indeed did happen and moreover was performed "by the Name of Jesus Christ of Nazareth, whom you crucified, whom God raised from the dead."

Then, citing the same prophecy that the Lord used concerning Himself, that is, Psalm 117:22 in Matthew 21:42, the apostle called the Lord Jesus Christ "the stone which was rejected by you builders, which has become the chief cornerstone." Then he added, "Nor is there salvation in any other." He meant that Jesus, Whom they crucified, became the cornerstone of the new edifice of the kingdom of God on earth, and only by His Name can anyone attain salvation, because He alone is the Redeemer of mankind from sin, the curse, and death.

These words made such a strong impression on the members of the Sanhedrin that they did not know how to judge the apostles. They were amazed first of all by the unusual boldness of Peter's confession of Christ before the whole Sanhedrin. Effectively, he had switched roles with them, no longer the accused but the accuser, charging them with the death of Christ. They wondered at his boldness and his oratory, seeing that both he and John were "uneducated and untrained men." They recognized in them the disciples of Christ and were assured that they were continuing the work of Jesus, which was so abhorrent to them. At the same time, the presence of the healed man placed a seal of silence on their lips. They could say nothing to contradict the reality of the miracle performed by the apostles.

Having been placed in this difficult position, they sent out the apostles to confer among themselves about the best way of dealing with these unpleasant miracle-workers. They were seized with indecision, evidently as a result of everything that had occurred recently, beginning with the resurrection of Christ. It is possible that among them were people like Joseph of Arimathea and Nicodemus, and for that reason their decision was quite mild: all they did was forbid the apostles to "speak at all [or] teach in the name of Jesus."

Clearly, this was the decision of people much disconcerted by circumstances. "O the folly!" St John Chrysostom comments on this, and continues:

> Persuaded that He was risen, and having received this proof of it, they expected that He whom death could not hold, could be cast into the shade by their machinations. What can match the folly of this! Such is the nature of wickedness: it has no eyes for anything, but on all occasions it is thrown into perturbation.[11]

With amazing courage and boldness, the apostles both answered, "Whether it is right in the sight of God to listen to you more than to God, you judge." Moreover, they openly said that they could not stop preaching about events to which they were eyewitnesses. The Sanhedrin's fear of the people further prevented them from harming the apostles, and Peter and John were set free. Here we see the obvious moral victory of the apostles, but also the threatening signs of imminent persecution for their faith, which was to befall the apostles themselves and the first generation of Christians. The apostles' answer to the Sanhedrin gives us a clear indication of how to act when earthly powers require us to do something contrary to the divine law and our conscience: we must never go against God's law or the guidance of our conscience merely to curry favor with earthly rulers.

The Prayer of the Apostles, and the Pouring out of the Holy Spirit on the Faithful (4:23–31).

No sooner had the apostles been released than they "went to their own companions," to the house where the rest of the apostles and some other faithful were, most likely, praying for a positive outcome of the trial. All were inspired by the apostles' account, and the entire assembly, as having one mind and one heart, turned to God with ardent prayer. This is the first testimony about a common Christian prayer that we have. In this prayer, they first of all sought consolation and encouragement, surrendering the whole affair into the hands of God and asking God only for the boldness to continue preaching the truth. In connection with the Sanhedrin's threats, the foundation of this prayer was the words of David, who foresaw how earthly authorities would rise up against the Messiah and God Himself: "The kings of the earth stood up, and the rulers were gathered together, against the Lord, and against His Christ" (Ps 2:2). The Christians in their prayer applied this expression to the Messiah, Lord Jesus Christ, against Whom all rose up in this city of Jerusalem, so that, unbeknownst to them, they might complete what was preordained by the divine counsel: the redemption of mankind by the death of the Son of God.

The meaning of the rest of the prayer, according to St John Chrysostom, was as follows: "bring those words to accomplishment and show that they imagine vain things."[12] In other words, they asked that God show them that it will be impossible to stop the spreading of the gospel concerning the crucified and risen Messiah. Finally, rather than concluding their prayer with a petition to avoid persecution, they asked God only for courage and boldness to proclaim concerning Christ, "and that signs and wonders may be done through [His] Name."

Their ardent prayer to God was answered with a miraculous sign: "the place where they were assembled together was shaken, and they were all filled with the Holy Spirit." This miraculous shaking was a symbolic manifestation of the power of the Lord that will never leave His people helpless and powerless before enemies. Their petition was fulfilled at once, and having been filled with a special inspiration from the Holy Spirit, they fearlessly stood before the forthcoming sufferings for the sake of Christ. They saw themselves as strong and capable to speak "the word of God with boldness."

The Mutual Love of the Members of the First Christian Community (4:32–37).
The number of the Christian community increased more than twice in size after the miracle of the healing of the man lame from birth. Therefore, the author of Acts decided that now would be a good time to give a second characterization of the now-increased community to show that its inner state remained the same, that of the full oneness of mind and mutual brotherly love. The sharing of property also continued; therefore, no one called anything his own. The apostles continued to preach with "great power" about the resurrection of Christ. This did not mean that they preached only about this, but that the resurrection of Christ, as the foundation of the Christian faith (1 Cor 15:14), was the foundational precept of the entire apostolic preaching.

Among the first Christians, no one was in need, because those who owned land or homes willingly sold everything and brought the proceeds from the sale to the apostles, who helped all the needy from this common treasury. An example of such generosity was Joses of Cyprus, called Barnabas, which means "son of consolation," probably because he had a gift of consoling others with his speech. It is interesting that he was a Levite, that is, from the class of the ministers of the temple who were especially antagonistic to the Lord Jesus Christ. It is likely that the land he sold was in Palestine, because that land traditionally belonged to the ministers of the temple, the priests and Levites, as we see from the example of Prophet Jeremiah (32:7). This was the same Barnabas, well known in the history of the early Church, who became the fellow traveler of St Paul and was mentioned many times in the Book of Acts.

Acts Chapter Five

The History of Ananias and Sapphira, Who Hid Part of the Proceeds of the Sale of Their Property (5:1–11). Miracles Performed by the Apostles and a New Persecution by the Sanhedrin. The Apostles Are Imprisoned, Released by an Angel, Preach in the Temple. Answering the Sanhedrin, the Counsel of Gamaliel, and the Release of the Apostles After Flogging (5:12–42).

The History of Ananias and Sapphira, Who Hid Part of the Proceeds of the Sale of Their Property (5:1–11).
After the praiseworthy example of Barnabas, St Luke offers his readers an opposite example of moral perdition, even in this ideal community of first Christians. A certain man and his wife, named Ananias and Sapphira, having sold off their property, hid some of the proceeds and only brought a certain part to the common treasury of the apostles. They claimed that the money they brought was the

complete proceeds from the sale (see Acts 5:8). By doing this, they showed not only their avarice, but also their intentional falsehood and, most important, their hypocrisy, akin to that of the Pharisees. They wanted to appear to be as generous as the other Christians, even though they were not so in actual fact. This was the first stain on the holy community of early Christians, and as such, this action could not remain unpunished, and in the most severe manner possible, for the edification of all. The Apostle Peter found out about their subterfuge, doubtless by the inspiration of the Holy Spirit, and confronted Ananias with his sin, calling it the work of the father of lies, the devil: "Why has Satan filled your heart to lie to the Holy Spirit?" Peter categorized this action of Satan within Ananias in nearly the same words St John used in his Gospel to describe the influence of the devil upon Judas (see John 12:6). This made it evident how dangerous this sin of Ananias and Sapphira would have been for the entire early Christian community, if St Peter had not discovered it and excised it at the very root.

"While it remained, was it not your own?"—the apostle addressed Ananias. From this question we see that the sharing of property and assets was not forced on the members of the community but was completely voluntary. The sin of Ananias was the deception that he tried to accomplish, his decision to make his partial gift appear to be a complete gift. "You have not lied to men but to God." This phrase vividly indicates the divinity of the Holy Spirit, and His Personhood. Peter's words revealed to Ananias the depth of his moral fall, which he, perhaps, had not fully realized.

"Then Ananias, hearing these words, fell down and breathed his last." This was the direct punishment of God for the terrible sin against the Holy Spirit. The severity of the punishment is explained by the danger contained within this Judas-like sin for the entire community of first Christians. A single sinner was very dangerous for the others, because his sin could easily infect others. "Do you not know that a little leaven leavens the whole lump?" (1 Cor 5:6). This apostolic word explains the severity of Ananias's punishment. The sin of Ananias could have been fatal for an entire community, and therefore the rotten branch was cut off immediately, for fear of his example becoming habitual to others.

"So great fear came upon all those who heard these things." Probably all this took place in the context of a common Christian assembly, perhaps even a liturgical one, and such obvious punishment from God could not fail to make a deep impression on all. "And the young men arose and wrapped him up"—these were probably young servers who fulfilled various errands, as was also common in synagogues. "[They] carried him out, and buried him": they immediately took the corpse outside the city, at the usual place of burial, and buried him there.

Ananias's wife knew nothing about the events that transpired. When she came, about three hours later, St Peter accused her of participating in the deception of her husband. Desiring to give her an opportunity to justify herself and repent, the holy apostle asked her for how much they sold their property. She merely repeated her husband's lie. "Then Peter said to her, 'How is it that you have agreed together to test the Spirit of the Lord?'" In this moment, the young men returned, having buried her husband, and St Peter took advantage of this to tell her that the same punishment awaited her as her husband. "And they will carry you out. Then immediately she fell down at his feet and breathed her last.... So great fear came upon all the church and upon all who heard these things." It is interesting to note that this is the first time St Luke uses the term *ekklesia* (i.e., the Church) to refer to the early Christian community.

Miracles Performed by the Apostles and a New Persecution by the Sanhedrin. The Apostles Are Imprisoned, Released by an Angel, Preach in the Temple. Answering the Sanhedrin, the Counsel of Gamaliel, and the Release of the Apostles After Flogging (5:12–42).

Having completed the narrative concerning the events in the internal life of the early Church, St Luke again remarks on the characteristic way of life of the Christian community. Typical of this period were the many miracles and signs performed by the apostles "among the people," that is, among those still unbelieving, to attract them to faith in Christ. Typical also is the unity of the community, their life of "one accord." All those who believed in Christ remained together, even when praying in the temple, as a single mass of people. Their usual place was Solomon's Porch, a covered gallery near the main entrance into the temple, evidently comfortable for the Christians on account of its size. The other people held them in awed respect and even a little fear, and so they were usually left alone: "yet none of the rest dared join them, but the people esteemed them highly." In other words, the unbelievers praised them, revering their high moral and religious qualities.

Every day more and more people joined the Christians, both men and women. Especially amazing were the miracles of healing. If before a mere touch of Christ's garments granted healing, now even the shadow of Peter healed people when he was passing by. Christ's words literally became fulfilled in the apostles: "he who believes in Me, the works that I do he will do also; and greater works than these he will do" (John 14:12).

The amazing success of the apostolic ministry resulted in a new persecution against the apostles by the Jewish authorities. Just as in the past the Jewish authorities were inflamed with jealousy against the Lord, so also now "the high priest rose up and all those who were with him (which is the sect of the Sadducees), and they were filled with indignation." The high priest mentioned here is most likely Caiaphas, who was then the ruling high priest. The moral and religious corruption of the elite of Jewish religious society was so great that there was nothing strange in the high priests' belonging to the sect of the Sadducees, who denied the immortality of the soul and the resurrection of the dead. Josephus clearly attests that one son of

Hanan, or Annas, Caiaphus's father-in-law, was a Sadducee. It is possible that Caiaphas did not openly adhere to this sect, but secretly agreed with its views.

This time, the apostles were treated more roughly, with some even "plott[ing] to kill them." They were put in the common prison, like the worst of criminals. "But at night an angel of the Lord opened the prison doors and brought them out." The more severe the persecutions of the newly established Church, the more manifest is the miraculous help of God. By the command of the angel, immediately upon their release, the apostles fearlessly returned to preaching openly in the temple. This remarkable boldness and courage can be explained only by the grace of the Holy Spirit encouraging their natural strength, making them fearless. Then the apostles were brought before the Sanhedrin, but St Luke takes pains to emphasize that they were "brought without violence." So great was the sympathy of the people for the Apostles, the Sanhedrin feared that the people would intercede for them and begin rioting.

Their interrogation began with a formal accusation from the high priest: "did we not strictly command you not to teach in this name?" It is typical that not a single word was spoken about the apostles' miraculous release from prison. Evidently the judges guessed at the miracle, but intentionally ignored it. "You ... intend to bring this Man's blood on us!" They accused the apostles of trying to bring upon them the guilt of killing an innocent man, calling down God's punishment. It is as if they forgot how they themselves cried: "His blood be on us and on our children" (Matt 27:25).

In the words of the high priest, we seem to hear the voice of a reproaching conscience, the recognition of his own personal guilt, or, at the very least, a sense of the false position in which the rulers of the people found themselves with reference to this entire affair. Again Peter, on behalf of all the apostles, spoke in the same manner as before, only this time his words were even stronger and more direct: "we ought to obey God rather than men." Then he again powerfully witnessed to the divinity of Christ, almost in the same words as before, underlining the guilt of the Jews in killing the Messiah Who was sent to them, "Jesus whom you murdered by hanging on a tree." These words stress the personal responsibility of each member of the Sanhedrin, for hanging someone on a tree was associated with a curse (see Gal 3:13).

Peter's defense becomes a dreadful accusation against the Jewish authorities, and they "were furious and plotted to kill them." This evil intention was prevented by the wise counsel of one member of the Sanhedrin, the universally respected Pharisee and scholar of the Law, Rabbi Gamaliel. According to the Talmud, Gamaliel was one of the preeminent Jewish rabbis, the son of Rabbi Simeon and the grandson of another renowned teacher, Rabbi Hillel. He was the Apostle Paul's teacher, and according to tradition, himself eventually became a Christian and a preacher of the Gospel. The Orthodox Church venerates him as equal to the apostles, and commemorates him on January 4 and August 2.

Gamaliel began to counsel the Sanhedrin to "take heed" before they decide to do anything rash against the disciples of Christ. His thought was that the Sanhedrin needed to leave Christianity to the natural flow of events, because if it did not accord with God's will, it would naturally pass away. As proof of his words, Gamaliel offered two recent events. Two fanatics, Theudas and Judas of Galilee, perished with no help from the Sanhedrin, and their movement soon died as well. From Josephus, we know that a certain Judas of Gamala, also known as Judas of Galilee, rioted against the Romans in A.D. 6, when Emperor Augustus, having deposed the ethnarch Herod Archelaus, made Judea officially a Roman province and commanded a census that was to be the basis for a new tax code. The armed resistance was bloody and of long duration, but it was finally crushed by the Romans. The followers of Judas, known as the sect of the Zealots, later took part in the wars against Vespasian and Titus.

Theudas was a false prophet who called the Jews to independence when Cuspius Fadus was procurator of Judea (A.D. 44–46). Theudas's revolt was quickly dispersed, and he was killed. However, Gamaliel may be speaking of another Theudas, as the aforementioned Theudas lived later, having appeared only after the death of King Herod Agrippa I in A.D. 44, which is mentioned in Acts 12. In any case, Gamaliel uttered a wise consideration that the works of man are merely of human provenance, with only human strivings and goals, and God does not will them or bless them, so they perish on their own, for because they are sinful, they carry the seed of their own destruction within themselves. "But if it is of God," said Gamaliel (i.e., if there is God's will and His blessing upon this work, that is, Christianity), then "you cannot overthrow it," for no man can battle the omnipotence of God. In addition, any person who struggles against God's will is guilty of terrible sin (i.e., "to fight against God"). Gamaliel thus suggested that the Sanhedrin should wait to see what would happen.

For us, Gamaliel's motives present an interesting subject of discussion. The ancients believed that he was secretly inclined to Christianity. More recently, some commentators prefer to see in this counsel this rabbi's simple ambivalence or indifference toward Christianity. However, this cannot be, for pointless then would be the threat with which Gamaliel ends his counsel: "lest you even be found to fight against God." These are obviously the words of a man inclined toward Christianity, a man who already saw the power of God working in its favor.

The speech of Gamaliel, impartial in its external form, so impressed the other members of the Sanhedrin that they agreed with him, though not completely. They decided to flog the apostles, and having again forbidden them to preach, released them. This beating was the first persecution that the apostles endured for the sake of their beloved Teacher, and they accepted this dishonor with joy. Despite the prohibition, they continued to proclaim the gospel.

Acts Chapter Six

Choosing the Seven Deacons (6:1–7). The Preaching of Archdeacon Stephen (6:8–15).

Choosing the Seven Deacons (6:1–7).

"In those days ..." Although this is an inexact expression, it still indicates that relatively little time had passed since the imprisonment and release of the apostles. After the new moral victory of the church over its enemies, the number of Christians continued to increase. But at the same time, there was some disruption in the inner life of the community. This was an important problem, for it indicated inner division and lack of agreement among the members of the "single-hearted" community. "There arose a complaint against the Hebrews by the Hellenists." The Hellenists were the Jews who had lived in various pagan lands of the Jewish diaspora and spoke Greek, the cultural language of the empire. Sometimes, this label also referred to the proselytes, that is, Gentiles who converted to Judaism. The "Hebrews," however, were the Christians from among the Palestinian Jews who dwelled in their own native land and spoke Hebrew or Aramaic.

Every person received what he needed for nourishment and annual sustenance from the common treasury that was at the disposal of the apostles. The Hellenists, however, believed that their widows were being neglected "in the daily distribution." It is difficult to determine the reason for this impression. St John Chrysostom believed that the neglect was not deliberate, but rather a lack of careful planning, resulting from the constant growth of the now large Christian community. It is also possible that this was the arrogance of the Jews toward the Hellenists, who, whether they willed it or not, were still tainted by association with the Gentile milieu wherein they lived. These differences between two different factions in the early Christian community could not be completely eliminated even by the exalted spirit of Christianity. Those who suffered the most were of course the helpless widows, as they had no one to care for them.

Because this mutual disagreement threatened to cause a greater division within the community, the apostles took definitive steps to cut off the potential evil. They called together, evidently, the entire Jerusalem community ("the multitude of the disciples") and offered to put an end to this disagreement. As they said, "it is not desirable that we should leave the word of God and serve tables." The most important work of the apostles was the preaching of the word of God, and they easily could hand over to others the distribution of food to the poor. Therefore, they offered to choose seven members (a symbolic number) of the community, men filled with the Holy Spirit, because serving the poor did not signify merely ministering to their bodily needs, but rather was meant to tend to their spiritual needs as well. They needed to have wisdom to do their work wisely, practically, and intelligently.

"But we will give ourselves continually to prayer and to the ministry of the word." This is the most important work of the higher ministers of the Church.

This proposal was eagerly accepted, for it resolved the problem of the nascent division. Seven men were chosen. Of them, the most famous would become Stephen, the first martyr for Christ. After him, Philip is most well known, and he also is mentioned later in Acts. Only tradition speaks of the other five. Prochorus was at first a fellow traveler with Paul, and then he joined St John the Theologian as a companion and a scribe. He became bishop of Nicomedia and died a martyr's death in Antioch. Nicanor was killed by the Jews on the same day as Stephen. Timon became bishop of Arabia and also died as a martyr. Parmenas died before the eyes of the apostles and was buried by them. Nicholas was a proselyte from Antioch. The choosing of a proselyte was intended to satisfy the Hellenists. It seems, however, that he did not remain long at the height of his ministry, for his name is not found in the list of saints.

The apostles, having prayed, laid their hands on the chosen men and brought down on them the grace of the Holy Spirit. This was in effect a rite of their consecration. Because none of the seven who were chosen to be deacons (title derived from the Greek *diakonia*, meaning "service, ministry") had Jewish names, then it is probable that all seven, or at the very least three—Stephen, Philip, and Nicholas—were Hellenists.

Usually, this act of the apostles is considered to be the institution of the third degree of the clergy: the diaconate. In any case, it is clear from the subsequent account that these first deacons were not merely the treasurers of the early Christian community. They had other, more exalted, responsibilities: they worked together with the apostles in the work of preaching the word of God and building up of the Church. We shall later see in the Acts that they not only preached but also baptized (Acts 6:8–9, 8:5, 38).

These chosen men evidently proved worthy of the trust of the community and helped to dispel all the previous disagreements, because St Luke writes, "Then the word of God spread, and the number of the disciples multiplied greatly in Jerusalem." The power of the apostolic ministry was so great that even among the priests of the temple many converted. The expression "were obedient to the faith" shows the power of their preaching, because it managed to break the obstinacy of the priestly caste. This was a decisive moral victory of Christianity over Judaism.

The choosing of the deacons did not in any way prove the existence of democratic elections in the early Church. It is clear from Acts that the apostles themselves were free in making all the decisions, and in their actions, they were not bound to the will of the faithful people.

The Preaching of Archdeacon Stephen (6:8–15).

The apostolic ministry and the martyr's death of Stephen had such great significance for the life of the early Church that St Luke's account of these events is especially detailed. At first, we read a description of Stephen's personality: he was "full of faith and power," a man who "did great wonders and signs among the people." Evidently, he was remarkable, even among the deacons, for the abundance of the gifts of divine grace. Everywhere he sought the Israelites who had come from foreign lands to convert them to faith in Christ, and he even visited synagogues for this reason.

According to the Talmud, there were 480 synagogues in Jerusalem at that time. It seems that every foreign country or possibly even every big city with a significant Jewish population had its own synagogue in Jerusalem, so that the Jews from that locality who traveled to the city for the pilgrimage would have their own place to pray. These effectively were places where fellow countrymen would feel at home. Thus, St Luke mentions the synagogue of those from Asia (i.e., the Jews originating from the Western Asia Minor); the synagogue of those from Cilicia, as Tarsus, the main city of Cilicia, had a large Jewish colony; the synagogue of the Alexandrians, for two of the five districts of the Egyptian capital were almost entirely Jewish; the synagogue of the Cyrenians, for a quarter of Cyrene was Jewish; and the synagogue of the Freedmen, so called because they were Jews who had been taken to Rome as slaves or born in Rome into slavery, and then later given freedom by their masters. Apparently, Stephen himself, as evident by his name and manner of speaking, was a Hellenist, and so he preached in the synagogue of the Hellenic Jews.

He immediately encountered opposition, and many began to argue with him. However, "they were not able to resist the wisdom and the Spirit by which he spoke. Then, they secretly induced men to say, 'We have heard him speak blasphemous word against Moses and God.'" It is interesting that they managed to incite the same people who had been so well disposed toward the apostles and Christians in general. Here we see the cunning of the enemies of Christianity, who themselves did not want to persecute the apostles openly, but decided to use the populace by stirring up general hatred against the Christians, as blasphemers against God.

Just as during the trial of Christ, the people seemed thoughtless enough to believe this slander. Stephen was seized and brought before the Sanhedrin, which evidently gathered quickly in an extraordinary session. As during the trial of Christ, false witnesses were brought forward, perverting the words of Stephen. Probably Stephen spoke, or merely hinted at, the end of the Old Covenant with the coming of the Messiah Christ, but the false witnesses gave his words a different meaning. They accused him of saying, "this Jesus of Nazareth will destroy this place and change the customs which Moses delivered to us."

"To destroy this place," that is, the temple, was the same capital crime of which Jesus Himself was accused. Naturally, the eyes of all were directed at the Christian accused of such a serious crime. There was, however, no fear in his face, no despair, not even any animosity. His face was "as the face of an angel." Doubtless, in this decisive and solemn moment, he was given a special illumination of the Holy Spirit, and this transformed his countenance, making it angel like.

Acts Chapter Seven

The Defense of Archdeacon Stephen and His Martyrdom (7:1-60).

The high priest asked Stephen, "Are these things so?"—that is, whether Stephen acknowledges his guilt in the deed in which he was accused. Stephen responded with a long discourse in his own defense, in which he summarized the entire history of the Hebrew nation from Abraham to Solomon. In conclusion, he accused his own judges in no uncertain terms. The most important purpose of Stephen's speech was to turn the accusation of blasphemy back against his accusers. The essence of Stephen's defense can be found in verses 51–53. It is as if Stephen wanted to say that he does not stand before them as a blasphemer of God, the Law, and the temple, but as a victim of their own enmity against God and the Messiah, the enmity that they had inherited from their forefathers.

Stephen said that he believed in the One True God and revered His Law. However, his opponents always resisted God and His Law, and for that reason, Stephen was being judged. To illustrate this better, Stephan allowed history to speak for itself, expressing himself calmly and thoroughly. He began from Abraham, the father of the Hebrew nation, and then continued with his nearest descendants, the patriarchs. Even in these ancient times, some opposed God, especially in the story of the righteous Joseph, who, by God's providence, became a saviour of his people. To dispel any suspicion that he blasphemed Moses, Stephen spoke in detail about the history of the great Law-Giver, underlining his own deep respect and also reminding his listeners how often Moses's own people turned against him (v. 27–39).

From the Tabernacle of the first Covenant, Stephen turned to the building of the temple by Solomon. Confirming his view of the temple through the words of Prophet Isaiah (66:1–2), Stephen then boldly accused his own unrighteous judges, accusing them of grievous sin against the Messiah and God. The members of the Sanhedrin were "cut to the heart" at his words, and when Stephen spoke about his vision of the glorified Lord, in extreme indignation they "cast him out of the city and stoned him."

This majestic speech was likely written down by a secret Christian, perhaps someone like Nicodemus or Gamaliel. Subsequently, it could have been transcribed by St Luke.

"The God of glory appeared to our father Abraham when he was still in Mesopotamia, before he dwelt in Haran." This phrase seems to contradict the account in Genesis 11–12, because the Lord appeared to Abraham *after* he moved to Haran. According to Philo and Josephus, however, the Jews had a tradition that the first appearance of God to Abraham occurred in Ur of the Chaldeans before he moved to Haran. Because of this first vision, Abraham's father Terah moved to Haran together with his entire family, but he died along the way, and then the Lord appeared to Abraham in Haran to repeat the same command He gave in Ur (i.e., to go to the land of Canaan). This tradition is confirmed by evidence in Genesis itself (Gen 15:7), in which God said, "I am the Lord, who brought you out of Ur of the Chaldeans." This also is confirmed in Nehemiah 9:7.

"And God gave him no inheritance in it, not even enough to set his foot on." Even though Abraham came to Canaan or Palestine by God's command, he still had no land to give to his descendants. This is obvious when we consider that he had to buy a field and cave from the locals to bury Sarah (Gen 23). Stephen indicated that the gift given to Abraham—his inheritance, as well as the Promised Land—depended entirely on God's will. The bondage in Egypt continued exactly 430 years: Stephen merely rounds up the number. The expression "then He gave him the covenant of circumcision" is used to show the drawing up of a covenant was entirely the action of the free will of God, a gift to Abraham and his descendants. God is not bound by this covenant. He continues to do what He wills ever after.

Stephen called the sons of Jacob the "patriarchs," because they were the progenitors of the twelve tribes of Israel. "Becoming envious, [they] sold Joseph into Egypt." Stephen does not include the sin of envy by accident. He wants the Sanhedrin to understand that this same evil feeling was the reason for the crucifixion of the Lord Jesus Christ, Whose figure was Joseph who was sold by his brothers to slavery.

Stephen's subsequent account concerning Joseph is based entirely on the Book of Genesis, and his telling of Moses's life is also entirely from Exodus. That Moses was "learned in all the wisdom of the Egyptians" is taken not from Exodus (there is nothing about this in the Old Testament), but from a tradition, attested by Philo. Of course, nothing is unusual in Moses's receiving the highest and most multifaceted education available in Egypt as the adopted son of the Pharaoh's daughter. This education consisted at that time primarily of the natural sciences, together with magic, astronomy, medicine, and mathematics. All this earthly wisdom was intended to become an instrument in Moses's hands for the great work of serving the truth of God.

Stephen's expression concerning Moses—"[He] was mighty in words and deeds"—in no way contradicts the fact that Moses was "slow of speech and slow of tongue" (Exod 4:10). Even if he stuttered, this did not prevent his speech from being remarkable for the authority that is characteristic of any person with a mighty spirit. Stephen's indication that Moses was about forty years old when he interceded for the Hebrew who was being beaten is based on a tradition that Moses's 120-year life span was divided into three periods of forty years each—forty years at the Pharaoh's court, forty years in Midian, and forty years in the desert with the Hebrews on the way to the Promised Land. Stephen used Moses's killing of the Egyptian as a foreshadowing of his eventual deliverance of the entire nation from the bondage of Egypt, something that the Hebrews did not understand because of their lack of faith in God.

When telling of Moses's time in Midian and of the appearance of the burning bush, Stephen followed Exodus strictly. As did Moses, Stephen also called the one who appeared in the burning bush "the Angel of the Lord," whom the ancients believed to be the Angel of Great Counsel, the Word of God, the Second Person of the Holy Trinity. Then Stephen began to express the greatness of Moses in vivid language, describing him as a deliverer, a miracle-worker, a Law-Giver, and a mediator between God and the Hebrew people, at the same time stressing the persistent disobedience by the people of Moses and God alike. The fact that one of the ancient Hebrews rudely pushed Moses aside with the words, "Who made you a ruler and a judge?" was generalized by Stephen to symbolize the entire nation's fickle and stiff-necked spirit. God, however, placed this man, rejected by the nation, as not only their ruler and judge but also their deliverer. Stephen obviously made Moses into a figure of the Messiah, also rejected by the Jews.

Then Stephen cited a prophecy of Moses, in which he indicated the coming Messiah, whose prefiguration he himself was (Deut 18:15). Remembering the giving of the Law on Sinai, Stephen said that Moses received the commandments of God through an angel who spoke with him. In Exodus, the giving of the Law is ascribed to the Lord Himself, but Josephus ascribes it to an angel, which concurs with the Apostle Paul's words in Galatians 3:19 and Hebrews 2:2. It is possible that here again "the Angel of the Lord" is indicated, that is, the Second Person of the Holy Trinity. Even though the false witnesses insisted that Stephen did not cease to speak blasphemous works against the Law, Stephen here praised the Law, calling it "living oracles," that is, the words that contained active, living power.

Then Stephen rebuked the Hebrews for their disobedience of Moses, because they made a golden calf for themselves, in which is evident the influence of Egyptian paganism, whose pantheon included a deified bull named Apis. Referring to the prophecy of Amos (5:25–26), Stephen then rebukes the Jews for worshipping the "host of heaven" during the forty-year wandering in the desert. In other words, they worshipped the sun, moon, and stars. Stephen openly names the gods the Hebrews worshiped in the wilderness—Moloch, a Syrian and Canaanite idol who was a deified sun as the fruitful source of life of earth, as well as Remphan or Rephan, a Coptic name for the deified planet Saturn, itself a symbol for time worshiped by the Arabs, Phoenicians, and Egyptians.

Then Stephen defended himself against the accusation that he did not cease to blaspheme the "holy place" (i.e., the temple). He spoke about the holiness of the tabernacle and then about the building of the temple by Solomon. "However, the Most High does not dwell in temples made with hands," he reminded the Sanhedrin, then citing the words of Isaiah (66:1–2) that God is present everywhere and cannot be limited by a physical temple. By this prophecy, Stephen challenged the common assumption of ancient Judaism that the temple in Jerusalem was the only possible place for true worship of God. This is also what Christ said to the Samaritan woman: "Woman, believe Me, the hour is coming when you will neither on this mountain, nor in Jerusalem, worship the Father" (John 4:21).

Beginning with verse 51, the Acts describe the change of tone in Stephen's apologetic speech: instead of defending himself, he began to attack his unjust judges. With the zeal of a prophet, he pointed at the wickedness of these chosen representatives of Israel, especially in their becoming traitors and murderers of the Righteous One sent to them, the One foretold by the prophets, the Messiah. Stephen called them, as did the prophets, "stiff-necked," that is, obstinate, insubordinate, and self-willed, as well as people "uncircumcised in heart and ears." This was especially offensive to them, for the Jews were vainglorious about their circumcision, whereas the idea of "uncircumcision" was equivalent to impurity and paganism. Stephen reminded them that they always opposed the Holy Spirit, as expressed in their constant opposition to, and even violence against His chosen prophets. Finally, he accused them of not fulfilling the Law.

Hearing such strong accusations, they "were cut to the heart, and they gnashed at him with their teeth." Finally, Stephen, filled with the Holy Spirit, raised his eyes to heaven and saw "the glory of God, and Jesus standing at the right hand of God," which he immediately described aloud as a bold confessor, calling Jesus by the name that He Himself preferred—the Son of Man, in agreement with the well-known prophecy of Daniel (7:13–14). This was the last straw for the Sanhedrin. They assumed Stephen to be blaspheming against God, and they "stopped their ears" and turned on the confessor. Leading him out of the city, they began to stone him. This was a lawless act of maddened fanatics, as we do not see any official conviction given by the Sanhedrin, which would have needed confirmation by the Roman authorities. The Sanhedrin, however, sympathized with this fanaticism and probably incited them. The Roman garrison, usually not very large in Jerusalem, probably would not have been able to stop this sudden gathering of maddened fanatics. The local procurator lived in Caesaria, and time would have been needed to inform him and to call for the needed reinforcements.

"The witnesses laid down their clothes at the feet of a young man named Saul." By the Law, the witnesses of a crime had to cast the first stones at the one they accused. They took off their wide Eastern-style outer garments so that they would not become entangled in them as they cast the stones. Saul later became the great apostle to the Gentiles, St Paul.

As he was being stoned, Stephen uttered a twofold prayer for himself and for his killers. This was the same prayer that the crucified Christ uttered to His Father from the Cross. "And when he had said this, he fell asleep," that is, the author of the Acts compares his death with a gentle falling asleep.

Acts Chapter Eight

The First Great Persecution of the Church After Stephen's Martyrdom (8:1–4). The Planting of the Church in Samaria by Deacon Philip and the Baptism of Simon Magus (8:5–13). The Apostles Peter and John in Samaria and Simon Magus (8:14–25). The Baptism of the Ethiopian Eunuch (8:26–40).

The First Great Persecution of the Church After Stephen's Martyrdom (8:1–4).

The death of Stephen was not an isolated incident. It opened a great persecution of the Church in Jerusalem that lasted for some time, although how long exactly is not clear. Tradition tells us that another deacon, Nicanor, was martyred on the same day as Stephen, and with him two thousand Christians.[13] The entire community, except for the apostles, dispersed, following the command of the Lord to avoid persecution (Matt 10:23). They fled to other cities in Judea and Samaria. The apostles considered the Holy City to be the center of the new Kingdom of God on earth, and so did not think it possible to leave Jerusalem.

Apparently, it were not the Christians who buried Stephen—they would not dare to do so—but "devout men" from among the Jews, secretly sympathetic to the Christians, who had the courage of Joseph of Arimathea and Nicodemus. St Luke opposes these virtuous Jews to the fanatical persecutors of Christianity, among whom was Saul, who would enter "every house, and [drag] off men and women, committing them to prison." Evidently, Saul was a tool of the Sanhedrin, given authority to act in this way. He admitted as much in his Epistle to the Galatians (1:13).

The Planting of the Church in Samaria by Deacon Philip and the Baptism of Simon Magus (8:5–13).

The hatred of the enemies of Christ led to an even greater spread of the Christian faith. The dispersed Christians everywhere sowed the seeds of Christ's teachings. From Acts 11:19, it is evident that they reached as far as Phoenicia, Cyprus, and Antioch. Therefore, from the very beginning, the wonderful words of Tertullian, "the blood of the martyrs is the seed [of the Church],"[14] were already proving to be true. The author of the Acts first reports about the conversion of Samarians as a result of deacon Philip's preaching.

This Philip was one of the deacons, and not the Apostle Philip of the Twelve, which is made obvious by the fact that the Samaritans needed the Apostles Peter and John to lay hands on them and call down the Spirit. Deacon Philip apparently had a home and family in Caesaria. After the beginning of the persecution, he decided to travel back to Caesaria. On the way, he stopped in the city of Samaria, which was renamed by Herod the Great as Sebaste. Seeing the miracles performed by Philip, the people joyfully listened to his preaching. Among those converted and baptized was a certain Simon Magus who until that time was famous in the city for his works of sorcery.

St Justin Martyr wrote at length about Simon Magus, calling him a Samaritan from the village of Gitta.[15] But he was not a magus or a sage in a positive sense, like the Magi from Persia who came to worship the Christ Child. He was a black magician, a sorcerer. During this time, according to various Roman and Greek sources, many such magi, having some knowledge of the powers of nature (still not very well understood at the time), presented themselves as superhuman. By healing certain illnesses, by using charms, by soothsaying, or even by simple mountebanks' tricks, they had such an effect on the ignorant masses that the people believed that they communed with "higher powers." Thus, it was said of Simon Magus that "this man is the great power of God."

This expression reminds us of Gnosticism, a later heresy that mixed Christian teachings with pagan notions. Central to Gnosticism was the teaching of the so-called *aeons*, the emanations of the *pleroma* (fullness) of divinity. Apparently, Simon identified himself with such an *aeon*, and the people, being fascinated by this, believed him. But the power of Philip's preaching was so great, and the miracles he performed were so astounding, that the people believed in Christ. They abandoned their fascination with Simon and were baptized. Simon himself was also baptized, but judging by his later history, his conversion was not genuine. Impressed by the miracles of Philip, he apparently hoped to acquire the power to perform similar miracles, thereby earning even greater glory and influence over the people.

The Apostles Peter and John in Samaria and Simon Magus (8:14–25).
The baptism of the Samaritans was such a momentous event, because these were the first people that became Christians without the mediation of Judaism. Moreover, they were converted by a Hellenist preacher. The apostles considered this event to be so significant that they immediately sent Peter and John to lay hands on the converts and call down the grace of the Holy Spirit upon them. Here it is important to note that the Apostles Peter and John *were sent* by the other apostles. In other words, it is clear that they did not consider themselves to be more powerful than the whole assembly of apostles, but rather were themselves responsible to fulfill the commission entrusted to them by the whole apostolic college. In other words, the assembly of the apostles functioned as a single body in which the individual members had equal status.

The laying on of hands in this case was the second of the mysteries, which later began to be performed by chrismation. Philip could not perform this sacrament, because he was only a deacon. "And when Simon saw that through the laying on of the apostles' hands the Holy Spirit was given, he offered them money." Evidently, the calling down of the Spirit was accompanied by some visible signs that Simon noticed. This makes it obvious that Simon himself, even though already baptized, was not found worthy of receiving the Holy Spirit, for if he had, such an action on his part would not have been possible. Possibly, his turn for the laying on of hands had not yet come, and he, not waiting for his time, rushed to ask the apostle directly not only for the gift of the Spirit, but for the authority to call down the Spirit himself.

In this request, the true deceitful character of the mage was revealed. Evidently, he saw the apostles only as bearers of higher magical power, and he wanted to own this unknown power himself to improve his skill as a magician. By offering money, he showed himself to be a man governed by avarice and other impure motives. "How is it that he was baptized?" asked St John Chrysostom. "Just as Christ chose Judas."[16]

"Peter said to him, 'Your money perish with you.'" This expression is not a curse, but rather an indication that Simon's moral state will lead to his perdition. It is a call to repentance. This sin, however, is so great, that St Peter did not even promise forgiveness, but only said, "Repent therefore of this your wickedness, and pray God if perhaps the thought of your heart may be forgiven you." Why is this? Because such a sin requires an especially deep and sincere repentance, and Peter did not see Simon capable of such repentance, as he said to him, "For I see that you are poisoned by bitterness and bound by iniquity."

Frightened by Peter's words, Simon asked the apostles to pray for him, but even this was hardly sincere. Tradition tells us that later Simon Magus was one of the most virulent enemies of Christianity, the father of all gnostic heresies. There is a tradition that later he appeared in Rome as a hardened enemy of the Apostle Peter, and by the prayers of the latter, was cast into the Tiber when he wanted to cross the river by levitating over it. His sin received his own name in the tradition of the Church: that of simony, which is the sale of God's grace or of ecclesiastical office for money.

The Apostles Peter and John confirmed the Samaritans in the faith by their preaching, and then returned to Jerusalem, preaching along the way.

The Baptism of the Ethiopian Eunuch (8:26–40).

After the conversion of the Samaritans, another important event occurred—the conversion of the Ethiopian eunuch, who was probably a "proselyte of the gate," that is, a pagan who received Judaism, but had not yet been circumcised. The angel of the Lord commanded Philip to go south, along the road from Jerusalem to Gaza. Gaza is one of the oldest of the five chief cities of Philistia, located southwest of Jerusalem, near the Mediterranean Sea. Having followed the angel's command, Philip met a man in a chariot, whom St Luke describes as an Ethiopian, a eunuch, and a lord under Queen Candace. The fact that he was reading Isaiah does not mean that he was Jewish, because he could have been reading the Greek translation of the Seventy (the Septuagint), something that is quite probable, given some particularities of the text as quoted in verses 32–33.

Eunuchs, that is, castrated men, often were placed in high government positions or as guardians of women's quarters in royal palaces. For this reason, sometimes important officials were called "eunuchs" even when they were not castrated. No castrated man could enter the community of God's people, but he could become a "proselyte of the gates," a second-degree proselyte. Most likely, this Ethiopian was such a man. He was the keeper of all the treasures of his queen, and so, according to Eastern custom, definitely castrated. At that time, the name "Ethiopia" referred to the country south of Egypt, on the territories of modern-day Sudan, Eritrea, and Ethiopia. This country was ruled by women, and just as in neighboring Egypt every king was called "Pharaoh," every queen of Ethiopia was called "Candace." The inhabitants of this country were possibly of a Semitic origin and spoke an ancient form of Ethiopian, belonging to the southern Semitic family of languages, but they were pagans. These were likely the Kushites often mentioned in the Old Testament.

By the inspiration of the Holy Spirit, Philip approached the chariot of the eunuch and, hearing that he was reading aloud a passage from Isaiah, asked him whether he understood what he was reading. With humility and childlike simplicity, this courtier admitted that he did not understand what he read, and he asked Philip to explain it to him. Taking advantage of the passage the eunuch had chosen, which was a prophecy of the Messiah's sufferings in Isaiah 53, Philip began to tell him about the gospel of Christ. He preached so effectively that as soon as they rode up to a body of water, probably between Eleutheropolis and Gaza, the eunuch asked to be baptized. All that Philip required of him was heartfelt faith, and as soon as he confessed Jesus Christ to be the Son of God, Philip baptized him.

It pleased the Lord to show both the baptizer and the baptized that they acted according to His will by performing two miracles. The first was the descent of the Holy Spirit on the baptized with no mediation from the apostles, as later happened with the centurion Cornelius. The second was that an angel of the Lord took Philip up, so that the eunuch no longer saw him and continued his way alone, rejoicing. Philip found himself in Azotus, a city about thirty miles north of Gaza. "And passing through, he preached in all the cities till he came to Caesaria."

Caesaria was apparently his permanent home. This was a large city on the coast of the Mediterranean Sea about sixty-six miles northwest of Jerusalem, and it was the seat of the Roman governor of the province of Judea. Until the time of Herod the Great, the place was a ruin of an ancient fortification, called Strato's tower. Herod built a city, calling it Caesaria in honor of Octavian Augustus. This Caesaria was known as Caesaria Maritima, to distinguish it from Caesaria Philippi, built by Philip under Mt Hermon at the site of a city previously called Panea (dedicated to the god Pan). St Luke often mentions Caesaria Maritima in the Book of Acts.

Ecclesiastical tradition preserved for us few details concerning the further story of this eunuch. We have no reliable witness concerning his name, but St Irenaeus of Lyons attests that this man "was sent into the regions of Ethiopia, to preach what he had himself believed."[17] Thus, after returning to his country, he was the first preacher of the Gospel to the Ethiopians, and he converted many people to Christ, including Queen Candace, whom he baptized.

ACTS CHAPTER NINE

The Conversion of Saul to Christ on the Road to Damascus, His Baptism and Preaching in Damascus (9:1–25). *Paul's Flight and Coming to Jerusalem* (9:26–30). *The Apostle Peter in Lydda and His Healing of Aeneas* (9:31–35). *The Apostle Peter in Joppa and the Raising of Tabitha* (9:36–43).

THE CONVERSION OF SAUL TO CHRIST ON THE ROAD TO DAMASCUS, HIS BAPTISM AND PREACHING IN DAMASCUS (9:1–25).

The spread of Christianity in Samaria and the conversion of the eunuch were the beginning of the spread of the Gospel beyond the borders of traditional Judaism. Soon, by God's providence, there would be an even greater expansion of the faith into the pagan world. For this purpose, the Lord chose for Himself a worthy vessel in the person of His most virulent enemy, Saul, who would become the great apostle to the Gentiles, St Paul. This is the same Saul who took part in Stephen's stoning and was so active in the persecution of Christians that followed (Acts 8:1–3). Not satisfied with finding Christians in Jerusalem alone, Saul decide to persecute Christians beyond the capital of the Jewish world. He asked the chief priests to give him a letter of recommendation, so that the synagogues of Damascus would give him the authority to persecute Christians there.

The spiritual state of Saul was such that, by human reasoning alone, there was no possibility of his changing his attitude toward Christianity. St Luke describes him as though he were a wild predator, choking on his fanatical hatred of Christians. With such predatory intent, he traveled to Damascus, the ancient capital of Syria, about 130 miles northeast of Jerusalem. From the time of the Seleucids, many Jews lived in Damascus, so that Nero's persecution of Jews claimed as many as ten thousand lives in Damascus alone, according to Josephus. The Sanhedrin considered all Jews in all countries to be under their authority in matters of faith, and so Saul, having in hand a letter from the high priest himself, could legally bring Christians to Jerusalem to be judged by the Sanhedrin as blasphemers and apostates.

The grace of God, however, worked a complete turnaround in this hate-filled persecutor of Christians. As he was approaching Damascus, a light shone upon him from heaven, so bright and blinding that he fell on the ground in shock. St Luke does not directly say that Saul saw the heavenly image of Christ in the radiance of this light, but the subsequent account makes it obvious that he did. Paul admitted as much in 1 Corinthians 9:1 and 15:8. Shaken by this light, Saul fell and heard a voice that said to him, "Saul, Saul, why are you persecuting Me?"

Saul was so unprepared for this miracle that he simply asked, "Who are You, Lord?" The Lord named Himself and added, "It is hard for you to kick against the goads." This was a folk saying, expressing the futility of acting against an insuperable power. It is as if God had said, "You are powerless, despite all your hatred, to stop the work that is accomplished by My divine power." This filled Saul with fear and trembling, and he humbly acknowledged the Revealed One as his Lord, and himself as His servant, and asked, "Lord, what do You want me to do?"

The Lord commanded him to go to Damascus, where he would be told what to do. The high priest and the Sanhedrin, apparently, gave Saul guards and helpers who also witnessed this miracle, although they all saw no one and only heard a voice. Saul ended up blinded by the light. This was partially a punishment for his persecution and partially a symbol of his former blindness to the truth of Christian teaching. With profound repentance, Saul did not eat or drink for three days, after which his fellow travelers brought him to Damascus.

"Now there was a certain disciple at Damascus named Ananias." Judging by the name, he was a Christian of Jewish background. Later, the Apostle Paul himself described him as a pious man who lived by the Law, and who commanded the respect of all the Jews in Damascus (Acts 22:12). According to tradition, he was later the bishop of Damascus and was martyred in Eleutheropolis. His memory is celebrated on October 1. The Lord appeared to him in a vision and told him to go to Saul and to lay hands on him to restore his vision. With childlike sincerity, Ananias began to dispute with the Lord, having heard rumors of Saul's persecution of Christians. The Lord calmed Ananias, indicating Paul's future calling: "he is a chosen vessel of Mine."

After Ananias laid hands on him, Saul's vision was restored and he was filled with the Holy Spirit. This was an incredible miracle, a special mercy of God. Similar to the centurion Cornelius, Saul was granted the gift of the grace of the Holy Spirit even before baptism, and the grace was called down by a lesser apostle, not one of the Twelve. "So true is it," said St Chrysostom, "that there was naught of man's in the things done [concerning Paul], nor aught was done by man, but God was present, the Doer of these things."[18]

"Immediately there fell from his eyes something like scales." Of course, we cannot think that actual, natural scales fell from his eyes—this was merely a sign of his inner purification. Then he was baptized, doubtless by the same Ananias. "So when he had received food, he was strengthened." "He was faint, therefore," said St John Chrysostom, "both from his journey and from his fear, both from hunger, and from dejection of mind."[19]

"Then Saul spent some days with the disciples at Damascus." This does not contradict Paul's own account in Galatians 1:17 that he immediately went to Arabia after his conversion. St Luke does not mention this journey from Damascus to Arabia and back to Damascus. This is typical of St Luke, who was scientific in his attention to primary sources, and records of the journey to Arabia likely did not exist when he wrote Acts. Verse 23, however, indirectly references such a journey:

"after many days were passed." The fact that St Luke first mentions that he was there "some days" and then "many days" implies the possibility of some sort of extended journey.

The ardent spirit of Saul was never dilatory, and having become a Christian, he wasted no time to preach Christianity in the synagogues with the same fervor with which he had heretofore persecuted it. The main point of his preaching was that Jesus is the Son of God. All who heard him were amazed by this sudden change. "But Saul increased all the more in strength," probably already after his return from Arabia, where he most likely gave himself to intense study of the Holy Scriptures in silence and solitude, now inspired by the Holy Spirit to read them in a Christian light. Now he proved, citing the Holy Scriptures, that Jesus is the Christ, the long-awaited Messiah. The power of his scriptural proofs were so great that he caused great confusion among the Jews. It was impossible to contradict his reasoning, and this caused the Jews to hate him so much that they decided to kill him. Day and night they kept watch over the gates of the city, waiting for the moment when he would leave it, so that they could kill him on the road outside the city, where there would be no witnesses. It also seems that they had exact information about Saul's plans to journey to Jerusalem. Saul avoided this danger by being lowered over the city wall in a basket by his disciples, probably out of a window of a house that stood adjacent to the wall. St Paul recalls this escape in 2 Corinthians 11:32.

Paul's Flight and Coming to Jerusalem (9:26–30).

"And when Saul had come to Jerusalem," this was, according to Paul's own words in Galatians 1:18, three years after his conversion. Part of this time he spent in Arabia. Paul describes his visit to Jerusalem in Galatians 1:18–24, and we must keep this passage in mind to correctly understand the account in Acts. St Paul, according to his own words, went to Jerusalem to see St Peter and remained there for fifteen days, and he saw none of the other apostles except for James, the brother of the Lord. From Jerusalem he traveled to Syria and Cilicia.

St Luke adds that Saul "tried to join the disciples," but they feared him, not yet believing in his conversion, and they refused to receive him into their assembly. This continued, of course, until Barnabas presented him officially to the apostles. According to tradition, Barnabas, who enjoyed the trust of the entire Christian community of the time, had studied under Gamaliel with Saul in his youth, and even after Barnabas become a disciple of the Lord, he continued to meet with his friend. They used to argue about Christ, but Saul remained obstinate until his conversion on the road to Damascus. Now Barnabas, having heard of Saul's conversion, took him by the hand, so to speak, and brought him before the apostles. It is unlikely that all the apostles remained constantly in Jerusalem, so at that point, Saul saw only two—Peter and James.

After this, Saul began to openly reside with the rest of the faithful in Jerusalem and to boldly preach the Lord Christ. His preaching was directed both at the Jews and at the Hellenists. Because he was born in Tarsus of Cilicia, he himself was a Hellenist, and so it is not strange that he tried to convert the Hellenists with especial fervor. As he argued with them, however, he inspired such hatred that they also tried to kill him. When the brethren—that is, the Christians in Jerusalem—found out about this, they sent him to Caesaria Maritima, and from there to Tarsus. Paul himself tells of this in Galatians 1:21.

The Apostle Peter in Lydda and His Healing of Aeneas (9:31–35).
After the conversion of the most violent persecutor of Christianity, the persecution faded and the churches in Palestine "had peace and were edified," continually growing in Christian perfection, living a God-fearing life. The greatest comfort for the faithful was the continuing pouring out of the Holy Spirit and the miracles that continued to be performed through the apostles. Two such miracles are described by St Luke.

"Now it came to pass, as Peter went through all parts of the country …" From this we see that the apostles had the custom of visiting various communities, doubtless to confirm them in the faith, to answer any questions, and so on. "He also came to down to the saints who dwelt in Lydda." All Christians were called "saints" at that time, because they were those being sanctified by the grace of God. Lydda was a small town near the Mediterranean Sea, not far from Joppa, to the northwest of Jerusalem. There, Peter healed the paralyzed Aeneas, probably a Greek, judging by the name, but probably not yet a Christian, because he is called merely "a certain man." It is typical of St Peter that he did not ask him about his faith in Christ, instead either seeing with his spiritual sight that he had faith or hoping to inspire faith by the healing. This miracle converted the inhabitants of the valley of Sharon—a fruitful and densely populated area stretching from Caesaria Maritima to Joppa—to Christ.

The Apostle Peter in Joppa and the Raising of Tabitha (9:36–43).
Then Peter went to Joppa, which is now known as Haifa, an ancient city on the shores of the Mediterranean. He raised there a "certain disciple named Tabitha." Apparently she was a widow, judging by the fact that much of her charity was directed at other widows. Tabitha is translated as "Dorcas," a name often found among the Greeks and in Josephus. *Dorcas* in Greek means "gazelle," an animal much associated in the ancient mind with feminine beauty and grace, for which reason it became a common female name, much like "Leo" became a favored male name because of the lion's masculine qualities. The dead Dorcas was laid "in an upper room" usually reserved for prayer. The other Christians were saddened by the death of such a generous patron of the poor, and so they called Peter, asking

him to come immediately. "But Peter put them all out" to give himself to prayer without distraction. Then Peter raised her from the dead with the words, "Tabitha, arise." This miracle converted many to the Lord. Peter "stayed many days in Joppa with Simon, a tanner," also most likely a Christian. The tanner's profession was considered unclean by the rabbis, but St Peter was above such prejudices.

Acts Chapter Ten

The Conversion of the First Pagan to Christ—Cornelius the Centurion—After St Peter's Vision (10:1–48).

While Peter was still in Joppa, the Spirit of God called him to begin the great work of spreading the Christian faith to the pagans. The first city in which a pagan converted to Christ was Caesaria of Palestine (Maritima). As mentioned, this was the residence of the Roman governor; therefore, a sizable garrison of Romans resided here, and these were more reputable men than mercenaries gathered from local ruffians. One of the local regiments, known as the Italian Regiment, had a centurion named Cornelius. From the subsequent account, we see that he was not a proselyte, but a pagan. He was remarkable, however, for his profound religiosity and morality. It is characteristic that no one but the Apostle Peter was called to this important work of converting the pagans, even though Philip the deacon resided in Caesaria.

From St Luke's words, we can deduce that Cornelius had come to acknowledge the falseness of paganism, and he tried to revere the true God in his own way. He expressed his reverence for God in charitable works and in the good order of faith and piety in his household. From verse 30, it also is evident that Cornelius even followed the Jewish custom of praying at certain hours of the day. During one of these hours of prayer, an angel appeared to him, commanding him to send to Joppa for a certain Simon called Peter: "He will tell you what you must do."

Cornelius immediately did what the angel told him and sent two servants and a devout soldier to Joppa, having told them everything, so that they could induce Peter to follow them. He considered it inappropriate to command Peter with the strength of his authority as a Roman commander. It was about thirty miles from Caesaria to Joppa. Therefore, those sent by Cornelius after the ninth hour (after 3 P.M. by our reckoning) could only arrive in Joppa by the next day at midday.

At this time—near the sixth hour—Peter went up, by custom, to the flat roof of the house to pray. There, he felt hunger and "fell into a trance," *ekstasis* in Greek, a state in which a person is as though outside himself. In this state, the external world with all of its impressions seems to close for the physical senses of a person, and another, invisible world becomes evident to his inner senses. The Apostle Paul describes such a state, which he himself experienced, in 2 Corinthians 12:2–3: "whether in the body I do not know, or whether out of the body I do not know, God knows."

In such a state, Peter "saw heaven opened and an object like a great sheet bound at the four corners, descending to him." In this sheet Peter saw all manner of animals—four-footed, slithering, and winged. "And a voice came to him, 'Rise, Peter; kill and eat.'"

Peter was probably on his knees in prayer. There were different kinds of animals on the sheet—both clean and unclean. The voice seemed to offer Peter to eat of any of them, not distinguishing between the clean and unclean. The apostle directed his attention to that aspect of the command, because it was so unusual. Therefore, he answered with vehemence, "Not so, Lord! For I have never eaten anything common or unclean." To this, the voice answered him, "What God has cleansed you [in opposition to God] must not call common."

These words were the essence of the entire vision, even though Peter at first did not understand it. The meaning and purpose of the vision are as follows: all these animals symbolically designated all of mankind. The clean animals symbolized the chosen nation of God, the Jews, and the unclean were the Gentiles whom God cleansed by the Passion and death of Christ the Redeemer. Therefore, in the new kingdom of God on earth, the kingdom of the Messiah, which is the Church of Christ, there is not and cannot be any distinction between Jews and Gentiles. All are equally purified by the Holy Blood of the Lamb of God, Christ, and all are equally worthy of entering His kingdom.

As we see from verse 28, Peter understood the meaning of this vision later. This vision opened a new era in the history of the early Church, the era of the conversion of Gentiles to Christianity without the mediation of Judaism. This vision repeated three times, a sign of its importance. Then the emissaries of Cornelius came.

Because Peter, who did not immediately understand the significance of the vision, was perhaps unsure of his course of action—a Jew, according to the law, could not accept the invitation of a Gentile—the Holy Spirit gave him a new revelation. "Arise therefore, go down and go with them, doubting nothing; for I have sent them." Peter did not immediately leave, but invited the visitors into his house and fed them, because their road was long. He left with them only on the next day.

Four days after Cornelius had his vision (as we see in v. 30), they arrived in Caesaria, where Cornelius awaited them, having gathered friends and relatives who also were devout. Thus, in the house of Cornelius a sizable group of pagans was ready to believe in Christ. Having met Peter, Cornelius bowed to him "and fell down at his feet and worshipped him." This full prostration was an extraordinary expression of reverence. It is possible that Cornelius considered Peter to be someone divine, and so Peter immediately stopped such worship, saying, "Stand up; I myself am also a man," the same as all men. In this, of course, we see Peter's extraordinary humility.

Having found in this house many gathered pagans, St Peter said that a Jew is forbidden from associating with Gentiles, but God revealed to him that he should not consider any person to be unclean or impure, and so he came without demur. He asked for what reason they asked him to come. In the Law of Moses itself, there is no direct prohibition for a Jew to enter the assembly of pagans, but the later rabbinic tradition, influenced by the Pharisees, developed a teaching that a Jew could not even enter the home of a pagan without being defiled. From the words of Peter, it is evident that he finally understood the import of his vision.

In answer to Peter's question, Cornelius told him of his own vision. Then Peter began to preach Christ. In Peter's sermon, there are three easily distinguished sections:

1. An introduction about the acceptance of all pious and virtuous people from all nations into the kingdom of God (10:34–35).
2. A short summary of the ministry of Jesus Christ before His death (10:36–39) and after His resurrection (10:40–42).
3. Reference to prophecies concerning the salvation of all in Christ (10:43).

The sermon of St Peter was suddenly interrupted by a wondrous and unexpected miracle—the Holy Spirit descended on all who listened to Peter. This is the only example in all of apostolic history in which the Holy Spirit descended on converts before their baptism and without any external action, such as the laying on of hands. This was a special sign from God for the instruction of those Jews who considered the Gentiles to be impure and unworthy of entry into the kingdom of the Messiah, at least without initially accepting Judaism. We find no more extraordinary gift of the Holy Spirit in the entire history of Christianity.

"And those of the circumcision who believed were astonished, as many as came with Peter, because the gift of the Holy Spirit had been poured out on the Gentiles also." The fact of His descent was undoubted, for the visible signs were the same as at Pentecost (10:46). Then Peter, having correctly understood the significance of this sign, said, "Can anyone forbid water, that these should not be baptized who have received the Holy Spirit just as we have?" There can be no obstacles to their joining the assembly of Christians through baptism without any preliminary acceptance of Judaic rites, as God Himself has chosen to grant them the miracle of His mercy and goodwill. After their baptism, Peter remained with them several days, instructing and confirming them in the faith of Christ. According to tradition, Cornelius later became bishop of Caesaria and preached Christ in several countries, ending his life as a martyr. He is commemorated on September 13.

Acts Chapter Eleven

The Circumcised Rebuke Peter for His Association with the Uncircumcised. Peter's Explanation (11:1–18). The Preaching of Christianity Outside Palestine, Especially in Antioch (11:19–21). Barnabas and Saul in Antioch (11:22–26). A Prophecy of a Coming Famine and Relief for the Christians in Judea (11:27–30).

The Circumcised Rebuke Peter for His Association with the Uncircumcised. Peter's Explanation (11:1–18).

The news of the baptism of pagans in Caesaria quickly spread throughout the Christian community of Judea and reached the ears of the other apostles before Peter had a chance to return to Jerusalem. The way that St Luke expresses this (v. 1) shows that this news was joyful to most apostles and brethren. However, this event—an unprecedented and unexpected one—could not go by without some confusion on the part of those Christians from among the Jews who persisted in their ancient prejudice against the Gentiles. When Peter returned to Jerusalem, the circumcised—that is, the Christians from among the Jews—began to rebuke Peter for his association with the uncircumcised and for his eating with them.

This was the first manifestation of that delusion or even false teaching against which the Apostle Paul had to battle so vehemently (the heresy of the Judaizers). In this case, the Jewish Christians were not so much upset by the baptism of the pagans as they were by Peter's coming to the pagans, not the other way around. They were also upset that he lived and ate with them. The holiness of the Old Testament Law, according to their point of view, simply did not allow this. Afterward, this false teaching reached such a fever pitch that the Judaizers even required all Gentile converts to the faith to first be circumcised and perform all the ritual requirements of the Mosaic Law (Acts 15).

At this point, they did not yet require this, but Peter still had to defend himself. In his own justification, he described in detail everything that had happened to him in Joppa—his vision from God and the conversion of Cornelius. It was not by accident that St Peter brought with him six Christians from Joppa, who became eyewitnesses of the extraordinary miracles and who could confirm the truth of Peter's account. Peter especially emphasized that the pagans received the same gift of the Holy Spirit as the apostles had on Pentecost and that this was the fulfillment of Christ's promise given before the ascension: "you shall be baptized with the Holy Spirit" (Acts 1:5).

It is typical that, according to Peter, he had only "beg[un] to speak" when the Holy Spirit descended on Cornelius and his household, which made further catechization of the faithful temporarily unnecessary. With his account, Peter did not directly answer the issues raised by the Jewish Christians, but he showed them the will of God concerning the pagans as justification for his actions. If God accepted the Gentiles into His church with such obvious and extraordinary signs, how could he, a mere man, not treat them as brothers, live, and eat with them?

This account calmed them, and his interlocutors even began to praise God for His mercy to the pagans. These rebukes from the Jewish Christians are interesting in the sense that no one would have dared rebuke Peter thus if he were the "vicar of Christ on earth," the "prince of the apostles," the "infallible head of the Church," as the Roman Catholics claim.[20] If he were, he simply could have indicated his authority as enough of a reason for him to act the way that he did.

The Preaching of Christianity Outside Palestine, Especially in Antioch (11:19–21).

In the words of St John Chrysostom, "The persecution turned out to be of no slight benefit [to the preaching of the Gospel] ... If they had made it their express study how best to establish the Church, they would have done no other thing than this: they dispersed the teachers."[21] The Christians dispersed as a result of the persecution at first did not preach the Gospel to anyone but the Jews living outside Palestine in Phoenicia, Cyprus, and Antioch. However, later—possibly after the news of Cornelius's conversion had become widespread—they began to preach to the "Hellenists," in this sense meaning the pagans, not Jews of the Diaspora. "A great number believed and turned to the Lord."

Antioch was a large and flourishing city in northwest Syria, on the Orontes River, six hours' travel from the Mediterranean. It was established by Antiochus, the father of Seleucus I Nicator, the founder of the Seleucid Dynasty, as one of many Greek colonies in the East that arose as a result of Alexander the Macedonian's conquests. The inhabitants were largely Greek, although many Jews lived there as well. St Luke underlines the great success of the Gospel preaching among the Antiochians: "and the hand of the Lord was with them." Truly, Antioch became one of the largest centers of Christianity in the ancient world. In the apostolic age, Antioch was like a metropolia for all the churches established by the apostles among the pagans.

Barnabas and Saul in Antioch (11:22–26).

When word of this successful preaching in Antioch reached Jerusalem, the apostles sent Barnabas to Antioch, doubtless to prevent any possible confusion. He was to take on himself the direction of this new, large Christian community. They sent Barnabas because he was a Cypriot, as were some of the Antiochian preachers, and he could more easily enter into intimate and sincere communication with them. Moreover, he was "a good man, full of the Holy Spirit and of faith," remarkable for an especially gentle and loving heart. He also had a special gift of consolation with his words, for which reason he received the nickname "son of consolation." Having come to Antioch, he, apparently, saw nothing untoward and increased the number of faithful by his preaching.

Having introduced Saul into the company of the apostles in Jerusalem, Barnabas doubtless knew of his calling to become the apostle to the Gentiles, and so he considered it necessary to seek him out in Tarsus, which was not far from Antioch. He brought him into Antioch to help in the apostolic ministry among the newly converted pagans. They worked together for an entire year, teaching "a great many people."

Then we hear an important word from St Luke, that "the disciples were first called Christians in Antioch." Until this point, they were called "disciples," "brethren," "the faithful," or "saints." Most likely, this name "Christian" did not appear among the Christians, but was given to the followers of the Lord Jesus Christ by Antiochian gentiles. Not knowing the dogmatic or religio-historical significance of the name of the Messiah, they accepted *Christos*, the Greek translation of the Hebrew word, *mashiach* (Messiah), as the Messiah's proper name and so named His "party" after His name, in the same way as the followers of Herod were called "Herodians," the followers of Caesar were called "Caesarians," and the followers of Pompey were called "Pompeians." Thus, the followers of the Lord were no longer considered merely a Jewish sect, as they had been in the beginning. This also means that Christianity had been accepted by the pagan world as something independent that included both Jews and non-Jews in its number.

A Prophecy of a Coming Famine and Relief for the Christians in Judea (11:27–30).

It is touching that no sooner had the church become established among the pagans in Antioch than immediately the church in Palestine entered into an intimate and brotherly union with them. The mother of the churches (Jerusalem) sent its teachers to Antioch; in return, the Antiochian Christians came to the aid of their brothers in Judea during a famine. St Luke tells how prophets from Jerusalem came to Antioch. Among them was a certain Agabus who warned of a coming famine. The Antiochian Christians decided to gather aid for the Christians in Judea. Whether this was done immediately or later, after the famine began, is not clear, but in any case, the touching brotherly love and unity among Christians coming from vastly different backgrounds—pagan and Jewish—is evident. Truly they were now one united Church of Christ.

This terrible famine did occur, as St Luke tells, during the reign of Caesar Claudius (reigned A.D. 41–54), who was the emperor to follow Caligula. During his reign, several famines raged in various parts of the Roman Empire. According to Josephus, there was a terrible famine in all of Palestine around A.D. 44, as well as another one in Italy and other outlying provinces in A.D. 50.

The aid was sent to "elders" (in the Russian translation, this word is rendered *presbyters*) through Barnabas and Saul. Here we see for the first time the title "presbyter." As we will see later in Acts (15:2, 4, 6, 22, 23; 20:17) and in some epistles

(Titus 1:4; 1 Tim 5:17, 19), these were leaders in the Apostolic Church, directing the Christian communities. They were pastors and teachers, as well as performer of the sacraments (see Acts 20:17, 28; Eph 4:11; 1 Pet 5:1; 1 Jas 5:22). They were consecrated to their service by the laying on of hands by the apostles (Acts 14:23) and bishops (1 Tim 5:22). In some cities with especially large Christian communities, such as Jerusalem and Ephesus, there were several presbyters (see Acts 5:1, 4; 20:17). We have no Scriptural account concerning the institution of this position within the Church, as we do with the establishment of the diaconate, but we do see the custom of consecrating presbyters for newly established communities quite early in the Church's history (see Acts 14:23).

Acts Chapter Twelve

Herod Persecutes the Church. The Killing of James, the Imprisonment of Peter and His Miraculous Deliverance (12:1–18). Herod's Death (12:19–23). Barnabas and Saul Return to Antioch (12:24–25).

Herod Persecutes the Church. The Killing of James, the Imprisonment of Peter and His Miraculous Deliverance (12:1–18).

While Barnabas and Saul, sent with aid to Judea, remained there, the calm of the Church was destroyed by a new persecution instigated by King Herod Agrippa I. He was the son of Aristobulus and Bernice, the grandson of Herod the Great, the nephew of Herod Antipas of Galilee (who killed St John the Baptist). Born ca. 10 B.C. and educated in Rome, he received from Caius Caligula the tetrarchy of his dead uncle Philip, as well as the tetrarchy of Lisanius, receiving the title "king." Later, he also received the tetrarchy of his other uncle, Herod Antipas. Finally, Emperor Claudius joined Judea and Samaria under Herod's rule, and so Herod Agrippa I, like his grandfather Herod the Great, became the king over all Palestine. Thus, the independent Roman province of Palestine had effectively ceased to exist.

Herod was a cunning man but a rash and wasteful leader. Having been educated in Rome, he hardly believed in Judaism, and yet he frivolously began a persecution against Christians to please the Jews. In other words, he persecuted Christianity only to curry favor with the elites of Jewish society, who hated Christians. The representatives of Jewish ecclesiastical authority, seeing this new king's desire to please and knowing how the Roman authority preferred him, realized they had a good opportunity to crush the ever-growing influence of Christianity.

In effect, this is the first time that the Jewish ecclesiastical authority openly allied with a pagan secular authority with the intention of destroying Christianity. The persecution began with the beheading of James, the brother of John, by the sword. A few days before Passover, the king ordered that Peter be seized and that a strict watch be kept over him, so that after Passover he could arrange a spectacle of Peter's execution. A lover of such spectacles (he was raised in Rome), the king wanted to please the local population with a public execution.

"Constant prayer was offered to God for him by the church." St Luke takes pains to underline that the following miraculous deliverance of Peter from prison was a result of the prayer of the whole Church. Four squads of soldiers guarded Peter, and he was chained directly to two of them, sleeping between them. If one were to reason in a worldly fashion, there truly was no hope for escape. The guards were changed constantly, and two were chained to Peter, while two more guarded the exit. On the eve of the day on which Peter was to be executed, an angel of the Lord suddenly appeared before him, and the dark prison was filled with light.

Peter, who committed his life entirely to God's will, was calmly asleep on the eve of his own death. The angel, having pushed him in the side, woke him up and commanded him to follow. The unexpectedness and extraordinary nature of the event brought Peter to such a state that he thought he was dreaming. In this state, he passed all the guards who stood at the door to his cell and then passed the guards who watched the exit to the prison. When he and the angel approached the exit doors, the doors opened of their own accord, and Peter, led by the angel, came out into the street. Only then, when they had walked down an entire street and the angel suddenly disappeared, did Peter understand that everything that had happened was not a dream, but reality. He thanked God for deliverance, and for destroying the hopes of Herod and the Jewish leaders to crush Christianity by killing a leader of the apostles, one who was the greatest in word and deed before God and man.

Having assured himself that he was truly free, Peter looked around to figure out where he was. He then came to the house of Mary, the mother of John, "whose surname was Mark." The traditions concerning this John-Mark differ. One tradition, supported by Blessed Theophylact, considers this Mark to be the same person as the evangelist and Mark the nephew of Barnabas. Another tradition, written down in the *Lives of the Saints* of St Dimitry of Rostov under January 4, says that this Mark is neither the evangelist nor the nephew of Barnabas, but a third person entirely. Yet a third tradition considers him to be Barnabas's nephew, but not the evangelist. In any case, this house contained many who prayed for Peter's deliverance. When Peter knocked on the gates, a servant girl named Rhoda came out to see who it was. Having recognized Peter's voice, in her joy she forgot to open the gates, and instead ran to tell everyone the news.

This news seemed so incredible to many that they were ready to consider Rhoda mad. Others said that it could be Peter's angel. This supposition proves that even from the beginning of the Church's history, a teaching existed about guardian angels who care for the salvation of each individual person, on whom they are bestowed at baptism (see Matt 18:10 and Heb 1:14). When, after Peter's second knock, the doors finally were opened, everyone saw him and was amazed. Having told the assembled of his miraculous escape, Peter commanded that James be told (the brother of the Lord, because he presided over the Jerusalem church) as well as the brethren.

Then Peter "departed and went to another place." What this place was, St Luke does not say. According to tradition, however, Peter was in Rome during the early years of Claudius's reign. This fits exactly with the time of the first persecution, which was most likely A.D. 44, after the Jewish Passover and in the fourth year of Claudius's reign. Peter is no longer mentioned in Acts until the Council of Jerusalem, which would convene in A.D. 51 (Acts 15).

We can easily imagine the horror of the soldiers when they realized that Peter had escaped. When all searches had proven futile, Herod Agrippa I ordered that all the guards be executed, and he left to go to Caesaria. Immediately after this, St Luke describes the terrible punishment of God over the persecutors of His Church. Herod Agrippa was for some reason angry with the residents of Tyre and Sidon. Because their trade depended on Herod Agrippa—the lands under his rule were the major trading posts where the Phoenicians bought bread, which they did not bake on their own—it was in their best interests to avoid quarreling with Herod. Therefore, they sent a delegation to Herod Agrippa to ask for a continuation of peaceful relations. With the help of the king's chamberlain, Blastus, they were given an audience with the king. This chamberlain, or "personal aide," was the *prefectus cubiculi*, the most important servant at court, the keeper of the treasury and himself a noble. He usually had significant influence at court. Judging by his name, we can assume that Herod Agrippa brought him from Rome, where he had lived before becoming king.

Herod's Death (12:19–24).

On the day of the audience, Herod Agrippa bedecked himself in his full regalia, which, according to Josephus, was made of pure silver.[22] He then sat on his elevated throne, perhaps in an auditorium, for many people were present. The people, impressed with this kingly display, began to flatter Herod Agrippa, saying "the voice of a god and not of a man." Most likely, these words came from the lips of pagans, not Jews, who would have never dared utter any such thing. But the angel of the Lord struck down the foolish proud man, doubtless because he did nothing to stop the blasphemous cries, enjoying them instead. Herod was struck with such a terrible disease that he basically was eaten alive by worms and died. Josephus described Herod Agrippa's death in detail.[23] Despite the persecutions of Herod Agrippa, "the word of God grew and multiplied."

Barnabas and Saul Return to Antioch (12:25).

Barnabas and Saul, having distributed aid to those suffering from famine in Judea, returned to Antioch, and they took John-Mark with them.

PART II

CHAPTER 4

The Church of Christ Among the Gentiles

ACTS CHAPTER THIRTEEN

Saul and Barnabas's Journey to Cyprus and the Conversion of the Proconsul, Sergius Paulus (13:1–12). Journey to Perga and Pisidia. The Apostle Paul's Sermon in the Synagogue (13:13–41). The Effect of the Apostles' Preaching on the Gentiles and the Jews. Persecution by the Jews (13:42–52).

SAUL AND BARNABAS'S JOURNEY TO CYPRUS AND THE CONVERSION OF THE PROCONSUL, SERGIUS PAULUS (13:1–12).

In the early Christian Church, a special gift of the Holy Spirit was evident—that of prophecy and teaching (see 1 Cor 12:28 and Eph 4:11). The Church in Antioch by this time had reached such a level of spiritual maturity that it had its own prophets and teachers. Among them, the writer of Acts places Barnabas first, most likely because of the respect he was accorded by the early Church and especially because of his work in establishing the Church of Antioch. Saul, on the other hand, is mentioned last, because he was the last to enter communion with the Antiochian Church, and his apostolic ministry had merely begun at this stage. St Luke also mentions three others who are not mentioned in any other part of the New Testament: Simeon, called Niger (probably a Jewish proselyte from Africa); Lucius of Cyrene, who is possibly the same person as the Lucius that Paul mentions in Romans 16:21 (compare 11:19); and Manaen, "who had been brought up with Herod the tetrarch," that is, Herod Antipas, the tetrarch of Galilee, not Herod Agrippa I. This is interesting, because being raised in the court of Herod the Great seemed to have no negative influence on this Manaen.

"As they ministered to the Lord." The Greek word used in the original text refers to the service of a priest in the temple; in other words, St Luke is probably referencing the Eucharist. It is also important to note here that they "fasted." Still, today's Protestants, who insist that they follow the Holy Scriptures alone, reject fasting. During this service, the Holy Spirit—probably through one or several of the local prophets—commanded to "separate to Me Barnabas and Saul for the work to which I have called them," that is, for a special work to spread the Church of Christ. As we see later, this was the calling to convert the Gentiles to Christ. Significantly, Barnabas and Saul had hands laid on them, preceded again by fasting and prayer. This was, effectively, their ordination to the apostolic ministry. Of course, it was not the entire community that laid hands on Barnabas and Saul, but the presbyters of the church, and this laying on of hands gave the future apostles a special gift of grace that would be necessary for the success of their work.

They then left on their first journey, accompanied by John-Mark, who was assigned to help and serve them, to baptize the newly converted, and to perform other secondary tasks. Their first destination was Cyprus, the Mediterranean island nearest to Antioch. This was also the most appropriate place to begin a lasting relationship with the rest of the pagan world. First of all, Barnabas was a Cypriot, and many Jews lived on the island. Second, because of the island's placement, the new apostles would have a much easier chance to encounter Gentiles than on the mainland; as sea traders, the locals had many contacts with the mainland, especially with the southern provinces of Asia Minor, where the apostles would travel next.

To travel from Antioch to Cyprus, the apostles had to go by Seleucia, a small port town near the mouth of the Orontes River. Here they boarded a ship and sailed to Cyprus, disembarking on the eastern shore near the city of Salamis. Because Barnabas was a Cypriot Jew, the apostles began by preaching Christ in the local synagogues. Even later, Paul always kept to this rule to begin with the local synagogues, and only afterward to preach to the Gentiles. From Salamis, they traveled farther west and crossed the island until they reached Paphos, which lies on the western shore of Cyprus. This was a major city, the residence of the local Roman proconsul.

In Paphos, the apostles encountered "a certain sorcerer, a false prophet," someone of the same ilk as Simon Magus, named Bar-Jesus (which literally means "son of Jesus"). He was a Jew, although for whatever reason he also bore an Arabic name, Elymas, either because he was born in Arabia or because he wanted to give himself the air of an "Eastern mystic." Apparently, this sorcerer had the ear of the proconsul Sergius Paulus—whom St Luke calls "an intelligent man."

We can assume that this proconsul was not satisfied with the paganism of the time. Perhaps he kept this Jewish mystic near himself to find some spiritual fulfillment in his teaching and wisdom. Not satisfied with this Jewish mysticism, however, he desired to hear the preachers of the new faith who came into his city. Elymas, which literally means "sorcerer," stood against them, afraid to lose his influence over the proconsul. "Then Saul, who is also called Paul, filled with the Holy Spirit, looked intently at him and said, 'O full of all deceit and all fraud, you son of the devil, you enemy of all righteousness.'" Immediately, the sorcerer was struck blind.

This accusation, connected with the miracle, so impressed the proconsul that he believed in Christ with no vacillation. From this moment, Saul is not longer called by that name, but is always named Paul, the name by which history came to know him. The majority of ancient commentators believe that this change occurred as a consequence of the miracle and the conversion of Sergius Paulus, who became the first spiritual son of Paul's apostolic ministry. Saul, in memory of this important event, took upon himself the name of the proconsul himself, Paul. Significantly, from this moment, Paul, as one who revealed in himself a special power of the Spirit of God and became the greatest of the apostles to the Gentiles, is now always listed as first among his fellow travelers by St Luke. Until this moment, St Luke listed them as "Barnabas and Saul," but now he constantly writes "Paul and Barnabas." Other commentators express the opinion that Saul was his Jewish name, while Paul was the Roman name that Saul bore from his birth as a Roman citizen, a practice common among the Jews of the Diaspora. At first, as an ardent Pharisee, he was referred to by his Jewish name, Saul. Later, when he began his ministry among the Gentiles, he began to use his Roman name.

Journey to Perga and Pisidia. The Apostle Paul's Sermon in the Synagogue (13:13–41).

"Now when Paul and his party set sail from Paphos, they came to Perga in Pamphylia." Immediately, Paul is listed as the head of the mission. "His party" included Barnabas and John-Mark, as well as possibly a few of the converted Cypriots. Pamphylia was a coastal province of Asia Minor located north of Cyprus, and Perga was the capital of the region, not far from the sea on the Cestros River. For an unknown reason—perhaps it was weakness of character and fear, something that Paul had reason to complain of later—John-Mark left them and returned to Jerusalem. "But when they departed from Perga, they went to Antioch in Pisidia." This was the major city of Pisidia, a province to the north of Pamphylia. Having entered the local synagogue on a Sabbath day, they sat down, and after the reading of the Law and the Prophets, the rulers of the synagogues offered them to speak words of instruction to the people. Although there was only one leader in any given synagogue, the "rulers" mentioned are probably elders, that is, the members of the ruling council advising the leader of the synagogue.

Some commentators believe that these rulers offered Paul and his travelers to speak because they had taken the places reserved for rabbis. It is more likely, however, that Paul and Barnabas already were known in the city as learned men, even before they came to the synagogue. Then St Paul uttered a speech that summarized briefly and powerfully the history of the Hebrew people from the time of the patriarchs to the kingship of David, with the intention—similar to St Stephen's—of indicating the great benefits God granted to their nation. From there, Paul moved directly to the story of the Lord Jesus Christ and the teaching of the forgiveness of sins through Him, along with a strong warning against unbelief in Christ.

This sermon was directed not only to the Jews ("Men of Israel") but also to the proselytes of the gate ("you who fear God"), who had their own respective places in the synagogue. This sermon can be divided into three parts:

1. The introduction to the sermon (13:16–22) is purely historical in nature, which speaks of God's care over Israel from the patriarchs to David.
2. The main part of the sermon (13:23–37) contains the teaching of the Lord Jesus Christ as the Messiah foretold in the Old Testament, including the preaching of John the Baptist, the conviction of the Lord Jesus Christ to death, His crucifixion, and resurrection. Characteristically, like Peter (Acts 2:27–31), Paul cites Psalm 15, insisting that these words cannot possibly refer to David himself, but only to the Christ.
3. The conclusion of the sermon (13:38–41) is purely practical in nature. Here Paul tells of the forgiveness of sins to those who believe in Christ, and he warns against unbelief with the words of the prophet Habakkuk (Hab 1:5).

The Effect of the Apostles' Preaching on the Gentiles and the Jews. Persecution by the Jews (13:42–52).

Paul's sermon left a strong impression on the proselytes (whom St Luke calls "the Gentiles"), because they asked Paul to preach again to them the next Sabbath. It must be said that most of the ancient manuscripts omit the word "Gentiles" here entirely, so we may assume that some of the Jews also were included among those making the request, which is proven by 13:43, in which St Luke writes, "many of the Jews and devout proselytes followed Paul and Barnabas." Evidently, their hearts were touched by the grace of God.

On the next Sabbath, nearly the entire city gathered "to hear the word of God." St Luke does not give us this second sermon, but only its concluding words in verses 46-47, inspired by the fact that the Jews, jealous of the great success of the preacher, began to contradict and malign him, opposing his words. The presence of so many Gentiles offended the Jews, for they simply did not accept the possibility that Gentiles could participate in the Messiah's kingdom. Then Paul and Barnabas openly declared that without a doubt the Gospel must be preached first of all to the Jews, but because they themselves reject it, making themselves unworthy, it is completely justified to turn to the Gentiles, as this was even foretold by Isaiah: "I will also give You as a light to the Gentiles, that you should be My salvation to the ends of the earth" (Isa 49:6).

These words gave great joy to the Gentiles who believed in Christ in great multitudes—not all of them, it is true, but only those who "had been appointed to eternal life," that is, "predestined." Of course, St Luke does not here mean absolute predestination in the Calvinist sense, but merely is indicating that the Lord chose these converts, so to speak, through His foreknowledge of the positive inclination of their free will.

From Antioch, "the word of the Lord was being spread throughout all the region" of Pisidia. Some Jews were so incensed by this that they incited a few powerful women—pagan proselytes to the Jewish faith—to use their influence to persecute the apostles so virulently, that they had to shake the dust off their feet, in obedience to the Lord's command, and leave these recalcitrant people to their unbelief. Here, for the first time, Jews joined with pagans to persecute Christians.

The apostles then journeyed to Iconium, the capital of Lycaonia, east of Pisidia. In Antioch of Pisidia, the new Christians "were filled with joy and with the Holy Spirit," which shows that they, having firmly believed, did not despair at the persecution of their teachers. "This revealed the power of the Gospel," as Blessed Theophylact commented: "the teachers were persecuted and the disciples rejoiced."[24]

Acts Chapter Fourteen

Paul and Barnabas Preach in Iconium, Lystra, and Derbe (14:1–7). Healing the Lame Man in Lystra. The Pagans Attempt to Offer Sacrifices to the Apostles (14:8–18). Persecution and the Apostles' Return to Antioch Through the Cities with Newly Established Christian Communities (14:19–28).

Paul and Barnabas Preach in Iconium, Lystra, and Derbe (14:1–7).

In Iconium, the apostles again started preaching in the local synagogue and converted a great multitude of Jews and Gentiles. But here again the unbelieving Jews "stirred up the Gentiles and poisoned their minds against the brethren." Still, this did not prevent the apostles from remaining in Iconium "a long time," preaching and performing miracles. The people of the city became divided—some were on the side of the unbelieving Jews, others were on the side of the apostles. In any case, the hatred of the enemies of the apostles was so great that they planned secretly to stone them. Clearly, these conspirators were Jews, because stoning was the Jewish form of execution for blasphemy. Having found out about this plot, the apostles decided to flee to other cities in Lycaonia—Lystra and Derbe, located southwest of Iconium. The apostles continued to preach Christ in these cities and the surrounding areas.

Healing the Lame Man in Lystra. The Pagans Attempt to Offer Sacrifices to the Apostles (14:8–18).

For the first time, the apostles found themselves in an exclusively pagan society. The inhabitants of Lycaonia knew enough Greek to understand the apostles' preaching. Among those who listened to Paul was a man lame from birth. Seeing his spiritual disposition, Paul considered it proper to heal him miraculously. Apparently, Paul's preaching inspired this man to believe in the almighty power of the One Whom Paul preached. The pagans, of course, interpreted this event from their own point of view—they assumed the apostles were gods come down to earth, and they began to prepare a sacrifice, to offer to the apostles as though they were gods. Barnabas, older in years and more impressive in appearance than Paul, was assumed to be Zeus (Jupiter), in whose honor a temple stood near the city. Paul, who preached constantly and had the gift of the word, was called Hermes (Mercury). St Luke underlines that the local pagans exclaimed these things in their own "Lycaonian language." This is natural, because especially strong emotions often are expressed in the native tongue. What the "Lycaonian language" was is hard to say. Some consider it to be a dialect of Assyrian; others consider it similar to the Cappadocian dialect; still others believe it to be a dialect of Greek.

The priest of Zeus planned to offer the sacrifice before the gates of the city, because the city was blessed by the visitation of the gods. When they found out about this, the apostles tore their clothes, a sign of great distress at this blindness of the people. They dashed into the middle of the crowd that had gathered at the gates of the city, and they begged the people to abandon the sacrifice. Their speech was full of sadness, and yet they spoke with great tact all the same—"God … allowed all nations to walk in their own ways"—hoping to avoid offending them in their excited state. Nevertheless, the apostles still called their gods "useless things," telling the people that they should "turn … to the living God, who made the heaven, the earth, the sea, and all things that are in them." In other words, they made it known to the pagans that they could know this true God through His revelation in the natural world. These words of the Apostle Paul remind us of his words in Romans (1:20 and later).

Persecution and the Apostles' Return to Antioch Through the Cities with Newly Established Christian Communities (14:19–28).

"They could scarcely restrain the multitudes from sacrificing to them." Then something happened that could hardly have been expected and that shows how fickle a mob's mentality can be. If these incredible foreigners were not gods, then they were obviously the enemies of the gods, or so the mob reasoned. Jews who had only just arrived from Iconium and Antioch encouraged this line of reasoning. The offended pagans stoned Paul and "dragged him out of the city, supposing him to be dead." Again, the fact of stoning shows the initiative of the Jews. They stoned Paul, but not Barnabas, because Paul was the more effective preacher and the more hated by the Jews, who considered the former Pharisee to be their greatest enemy.

When the disciples gathered near him, probably grieving for his death—maybe they even planned to bury him—he rose up and entered the city again, which was, of course, a miracle in itself. It also shows Paul's incredible strength of will.

Paul then left with Barnabas to Derbe, located southeast of Lystra. There, they also converted many to the faith.

Finally, the apostles undertook a return journey to Antioch through all the cities in which they had preached—Lystra, Iconium, and Antioch of Pisidia—to confirm the faith of the new disciples and to encourage them in the coming grief and persecution for the sake of Jesus Christ, teaching them that "we must through many tribulations enter the kingdom of God." This teaching is fully consonant with the teaching of Jesus Christ Himself, Who called the way to salvation the narrow gate and the difficult way (Matt 7:13–14). In His parting conversation with the apostles, He warned them, "In the world you will have tribulation" (John 16:33). The way of grief and suffering is inevitable for anyone who desires to be saved, for by this path walked the divine Founder of Christianity Himself. Therefore, the Protestants who consider themselves already saved by virtue of believing alone delude themselves when they deny the necessity of personal struggle for salvation.

Moreover, the apostles ordained presbyters for every church, that is, they assigned local elders for each community, which resulted in good organization and the possibility of performing the sacraments. Before leaving every community, the apostles prayed and fasted, which again underlines the importance and necessity of fasting. As they departed, they committed each community to the Lord, His mercy, and patronage.

The apostles returned to Perga through Pisidia and Pamphylia. After preaching there again, "they went down to Attalia," a coastal city in Pamphylia near the mouth of the Catarrhactes. From there, they sailed to their own metropolis, Antioch of Syria, from where they began this first missionary journey. There, they gathered all the Christians together to tell them that all they did, they did not on their own, but "God had done with them," humbly acknowledging their own insignificance.

Acts Chapter Fifteen

Disturbance in the Church of Antioch, and the Apostolic Council in Jerusalem (15:1–35). The Apostle Paul Leaves for His Second Missionary Journey (15:36–41).

Disturbance in the Church of Antioch, and the Apostolic Council in Jerusalem (15:1–35).

The insistence of the Jews on the necessity of the Mosaic Law was deeply ingrained; therefore, it was difficult for Christians of Jewish extraction to agree with the thought that the Law was no longer necessary within Christianity. When Gentiles joined the Church of Christ, this question inevitably came up in Antioch, the first Christian community largely composed of former pagans. Missionaries arrived from Judea, insisting that circumcision was necessary for salvation, even within Christianity. The fact that the apostles would later send a letter concerning this issue not only to Antioch, but also to Syria and Cilicia, makes it obvious that these missionaries had gone to Syria and Cilicia as well. These missionaries ended up being the first Christian heretics—that is, the Judaizers. "Paul and Barnabas had no small dissension and dispute with them." Evidently, these missionaries found people in Antioch—probably converts from Judaism—who were willing to listen to their teaching. We must assume that Paul and Barnabas rejected the necessity of circumcision for Christian converts from paganism; however, because the disturbance in the community was serious, and the inner peace of the community was shattered, it was decided to send a special embassy to Jerusalem to resolve this issue, with Paul and Barnabas at the head.

This divisive issue needed to be decided by the apostles who were in Jerusalem. By this time, together with the presbyters, they constituted the supreme administrative and judicial power in the Church, similar to the Sanhedrin for the Jews. It is also possible that the so-called missionaries claimed to have the sanction of the apostles in Jerusalem. The embassy from Antioch was "sent on their way by the church," stressing the importance of this embassy, which aroused general interest and sympathy.

"They passed through Phoenicia and Samaria," which was on the way to Jerusalem from Antioch, and along the way, they spoke with the local communities concerning the conversion of the pagans, which "caused great joy to all the brethren." Because they were the representatives of the great church in Antioch, they were greeted by the entire church in Jerusalem, together with the apostles and the elders in a special, triumphant assembly, during which they told the Church in Jerusalem about the conversion of the pagans. "Some of the sect of the Pharisees" immediately stood up and expressed their disapproval of the manner of reception of the Gentiles into the Church. These were zealots of the Mosaic Law, and they declared, "It is necessary to circumcise them, and to command them to keep the Law of Moses."

To discuss this important question, the apostles and presbyters gathered a general council of the entire Jerusalem church. The Apostle Paul remembers in the Epistle to the Galatians (2:1–21) how fourteen years after his conversion (or after his first visit to Jerusalem), he attended this council and insisted that the rites of the Mosaic Law were not absolutely necessary for Christians. From this information, we can calculate that the Apostolic Council in Jerusalem took place in A.D. 51.

The question was essentially this: the Gospel or the Law? Christ or Moses? Grace or the works of the Law? Evangelical freedom or the yoke of the Law? The Apostle Paul later taught in his Epistle to the Galatians (3:24–25) that the Law of Moses was given only as a guide to Christ, and so after the coming of Christ, it ceased to be necessary, for the new Law of Christ replaced it. To consider the rites of the Mosaic Law as necessary for Christianity was the same as to consider the redemptive power of Christ's Law to be insufficient. If the Judaizing heresy had held sway, Christianity simply would have reverted to Judaism. This is why the Apostle Paul, to the end of his days, resolutely battled this delusion, and all his epistles are imbued with the thought that man is justified only by faith in Christ, not by the works of the Law. This thought unfortunately has been perverted by the Protestants, who teach that good deeds are not necessary for salvation, even though the Apostle Paul would never even think of maintaining such an idea. He insisted on the irrelevance of only the Mosaic Law for Christianity. "The works of the Law" refer only to the rites of the Law of Moses, not to good deeds in general.

After lengthy initial arguments and disputes, the Apostle Peter stood up to speak. He reminded everyone of the universally known conversion of the centurion Cornelius, who received the Holy Spirit in an incredible fashion. The Knower of Hearts, God, Who could not have been wrong in His consideration of the Gentiles as worthy of salvation through Christ, placed no distinction between Christians from among the Jews and from the pagans. Thus, Peter asked, "why do you test God by putting a yoke on the neck of the disciples which neither our fathers nor we were able to bear?" In other words, why do you want to force them to follow such a heavy Old Testament Law, with its countless ritual observances, when neither our fathers nor we ourselves were ever capable of following them all?

By thus characterizing the Old Testament Law, the apostle showed that the Law cannot justify man before God; therefore, it is superfluous for Christianity. "We believe that through the grace of the Lord Jesus Christ we shall be saved." This thought would be developed in more detail by St Paul in his Epistles to the Galatians (3:10), Romans (3:9–19), 1 Corinthians (1:3), 2 Corinthians (1:2, 13:13), and Ephesians (1:2).

Peter's words were so filled with authority that the entire assembly fell silent, and no more arguments followed. As the later history of Christianity shows, the false teaching of the Judaizers was not completely or immediately eradicated, and they continued to disturb the Church for some time, but in this council, it was defeated by Peter's words, and his adversaries fell silent. Calmly and quietly, without interruption, the council then listened to the witness of Paul and Barnabas, who told of the great signs and miracles performed by God through them among the pagans during their missionary journey. All this confirmed the truth of Peter's words; the conversion of the Gentiles to Christ without preliminary conversion to Judaism was the work of God. Consequently, the Christians from among the pagans should not be forced to follow the ritual observances of the Mosaic Law.

Then the Apostle James, the brother of the Lord, began to speak. As the primate of the Church of Jerusalem—and as the chairman of the council—he had the final word. His words were also authoritative because he had the reputation of being a zealot for the Law, receiving for this reason the name "the Just" not only among other Christians but also among the Jews. St James's speech can be divided into two parts. In the first, he confirmed the truth of Peter's words with a prophetic word. In the second, he offered a concluding statement for the council's deliberation. Especially wonderful was James's word that "God at the first visited the Gentiles to take out of them a people for His name." Until this moment, the Jews had thought that only they were the chosen people of God. Now St James showed that the Christians from the pagans were equal members of the chosen nation of God. As proof of his words, he cited the prophet Amos (9:11), in which prophecy God promised to restore the fallen house of David, so that it would rule over all nations that would turn to the true faith. This is clearly a prophecy of the establishment of the Messianic Kingdom of God on earth, into which not only Jews, but Gentiles also have entry.

In the second part of his speech, the Apostle James offered to exempt all converts from the Gentiles from following the Law of Moses, requiring of them only the fulfillment of that portion of the Law that is consonant with the spirit of Christianity, that is, the so-called commandments of Noah:

1. "To abstain from things polluted by idols," that is, not to eat anything brought as a sacrifice to pagan gods;
2. "To abstain from sexual immorality," that is, from sin of the flesh in all its forms: this is an especially important requirement, as this sin was the most widespread in the pagan Greco-Roman world and was hardly even considered a sin;
3. "To abstain from things strangled," that is, to avoid eating the meat of animals killed by strangulation, because their blood—that is, their soul—still remained in their bodies; and
4. "To abstain from blood," which was forbidden as food, because it was an abomination even from the time of Noah (Gen 9:4).

A fifth requirement—"do not do anything that you would not have others do to you also"—is found only in certain ancient manuscripts and St John Chrysostom does not refer to it in his commentary. It had the purpose of pacifying all disagreements, but it did not refer to the ritual observance of the Law of Moses, and so there was no need to speak of this so-called Golden Rule, which is a purely moral requirement. It also is not included in the official letter of the council intended to be distributed among the churches. Unfortunately, the logical connection of James's speech with his final word in 15:21 ("For Moses has had throughout many generations those who preach him in every city, being read in the synagogues every Sabbath") is not entirely clear.

St James's decision was accepted unanimously by the apostles, presbyters, and the entire community as the official resolution of the council. It was decided to send this resolution in written form to Antioch with an embassy consisting of Paul, Barnabas, Judas also called Barsabas, and Silas. This letter was probably written in Greek, as suggested by the Greek manner of salutation in the beginning and end. In this epistle, those who required circumcision and the ritual observance of the Mosaic Law were rebuked, while Paul and Barnabas were praised as people who were dedicated to the Lord even to the sacrifice of their own selves, and by the name of the Holy Spirit ("For it seemed good to the Holy Spirit, and to us"), the Gentile Christians were exhorted only to follow those requirements that were offered by St James: "abstain from things offered to idols, from blood, from things strangled, and from sexual immorality."

Those who were sent arrived in Antioch and read out the epistle in what was likely a triumphant assembly. The reading gave joy and comfort to those who listened. "Judas and Silas, themselves being prophets also, exhorted and strengthened the brethren with many words," probably in connection with the disturbance caused by this false teaching. Silas remained in Antioch, and Judas returned to Jerusalem. Paul and Barnabas continued to preach in Antioch.

The Apostle Paul Leaves for His Second Missionary Journey (15:36–41). After some time had passed, St Paul offered Barnabas to visit the cities in which they had established communities during the first missionary journey. But this initial plan soon changed. Barnabas wanted once again to take John-Mark as a fellow traveler, but Paul opposed this. The word used in Greek shows that Paul considered Mark unworthy of being taken on the journey a second time, because he had failed to remain with them during the first journey, a journey on which they were sent by the Spirit of God Himself. It is obvious that Paul considered John-Mark's vacillation to be egregious, whereas Barnabas was disposed to be compassionate. "The contention became so sharp" that they separated. Barnabas went to Cyprus with John-Mark, and Paul went through Syria and Cilicia, taking Silas with him.

We must not think that this was a quarrel. St Paul even later spoke of Barnabas with great praise (2 Cor 8:18), and it was ultimately beneficial to the mission that Barnabas chose his own sphere of activity. For Mark, both Paul's strictness and Barnabas's condescension were beneficial. As St John Chrysostom notes, "the awe inspired by Paul converted him, while the kindness of Barnabas caused that he was not left behind: so that they contend indeed, but the gain comes to one and the same end."[25]

As tradition tells, Barnabas continued to travel through various pagan countries after Cyprus. He traveled to Crete, Italy, where he was first in Rome and established a church in Milan. After returning to Cyprus, he so angered the Jews by his zealous preaching of Christ that they stoned him. His memory is celebrated on June 11.

Acts Chapter Sixteen

The Second Missionary Journey of the Apostle Paul. Paul in Lystra and Derbe, and the Circumcision of Timothy. Journey to Troas (16:1–8). The Vision of the Macedonian and the Journey to Macedonia (16:9–11). Paul in Philippi: the Conversion of Lydia and the Exorcism of the Prophetic Spirit (16:12–18). Paul and Silas Imprisoned, Their Miraculous Deliverance, and the Conversion of the Prison Guard (16:19–40).

The Second Missionary Journey of the Apostle Paul. Paul in Lystra and Derbe, and the Circumcision of Timothy. Journey to Troas (16:1–8).

St Luke briefly speaks of the events preceding Paul's arrival in Europe—his mission in Syria and Cilicia, then in Derbe and Lystra, and finally in Phrygia and Galatia. The purpose of this summary is to tell how Christianity began to spread to Europe and reached, finally, the very heart of the Greco-Roman world, the great capital of the West, Rome. In Lystra, Paul solicited the help of a certain Timothy. Timothy's father was a pagan, and so Timothy was not circumcised. Paul circumcised him to make it possible for him to preach among the Jews of that place, who were numerous. Among those already converted, Paul did not stop telling everyone of the decision of the Apostolic Council, and he called all Christians to follow that decision. This circumcision of his disciple showed Paul's practicality, for though he himself taught that "circumcision is nothing and uncircumcision is nothing" (1 Cor 7:19), in this case he did this "because of the Jews." In this, Paul was guided by his own wise rule: "I have become all things to all men, that I might by all means save some" (1 Cor 9:22). The Jews would never have listened to the word of God preached by an uncircumcised man.

Of all Paul's fellow travelers, we know the most about Timothy. Beginning with this moment, he became a nearly constant fellow traveler of Paul and is mentioned in the majority of his epistles. In 2 Timothy 1:5, we even find details of his parentage. When the apostle was in bonds in Rome, Timothy was with him. As we see in verses 2 and 3, Timothy was from Lystra. His father was a pagan, but his mother was a Jew, and so Timothy belonged equally, so to speak, to the pagan and Jewish worlds. Therefore, he was quite useful for the ministry to both.

Together with Silas and Timothy, the Apostle Paul went through all the cities of Pisidia, Lycaonia, and Pamphylia, where he had planted Christianity during his first journey. Everywhere, he read the decision of the Apostolic Council. The churches in those places grew and became stronger. From Pisidia, St Paul traveled to the inner provinces of Asia Minor—Phrygia and Galatia. Most likely, this was the time that Paul established those churches in Galatia to whom he would later write one of his most important epistles (Galatians), as well as the churches in Colossae, Laodicea, and Hierapolis, to whom he later would write the Epistle to the Colossians. From Galatia and Phrygia, the preachers planned to go to the western coastal provinces of Asia Minor, called "Asia" in general by St Luke, which included Mysia, Lydia, and Caria. However, "they were forbidden by the Holy Spirit to preach the word in Asia."

By the time they received this prohibition, they were already near Mysia, which is why they decided to continue to Bithynia, the northwestern province neighboring Mysia, but again "the Spirit did not permit them." We must assume that this was because they were intended for greater missionary work in Europe, which is why, guided by the Spirit, they passed Mysia by and went to Troas, a coastal town from which it would be easy to travel to Europe by sea. Here they received a definitive revelation concerning their new mission.

The Vision of the Macedonian and the Journey to Macedonia (16:9–11).

"And a vision appeared to Paul in the night. A man of Macedonia stood and pleaded with him, saying, 'come over to Macedonia and help us.'" Perhaps this was the angel of the Macedonian nation in the form of a man. Macedonia was during that time a large province of the Roman Empire, whose northwestern edge bordered the Aegean Sea. This Macedonian man did not specify the nature of his people's need, but it is clear enough. Mankind without Christ is doomed to perdition, finding itself in a helpless spiritual state. To preach Christ to an unbelieving nation means to help that nation extricate itself from imminent ruin. This is how the apostles understood the man's invitation and they "sought to go to Macedonia." Here, for the first time, St Luke switches his point of view to the first person plural, listing himself among the fellow travelers of Paul. He continues in this point of view, with a few interruptions, to the end of Acts, a personal witness to all that occurred. Thus, we can assume that St Luke joined Paul's mission in Troas.

Paul in Philippi: the Conversion of Lydia and the Exorcism of the Prophetic Spirit (16:12–18).

Having left Troas, the preachers traveled to Samothrace, an island in the Aegean Sea northwest of Troas, thirty-eight miles from the shore of Thrace, which was already Europe proper. From here, they came on the next day to Neapolis, a coastal city at the mouth of the Struma River, which at that time was part of Thrace. This was the first European city in which Paul stepped foot (today's Kavala in Greece). From there, they immediately traveled to Philippi, a city of Macedonia proper. It lay not far from Neapolis, about eight miles to the northwest. Philip of Macedon, Alexander the Great's father, built the city on the place of the village of Krenides. Julius Caesar established a Roman colony there. So few Jews were living there that there was not even a synagogue. Therefore, the local Jewish population, according to the Jewish custom, met outside the city near the banks of the Krenides River to pray. This place was perhaps separated by a wall, but there was no permanent building there.

On the Sabbath, the preachers went there and sat down to speak with some of the assembled women. Most likely there were no men there at all, but only the Jewish wives of pagan husbands. Therefore, Paul did not speak at length, as was the custom in synagogues and large assembles, but only held an informal discussion with them. This discussion influenced a certain Lydia—"a seller of purple from the city of Thyatira"—to turn to Christ and accept baptism, along with her entire household. Thyatira was a Macedonian colony in Lydia, a province of Asia Minor. It is likely that Lydia herself was a Macedonian proselyte and that she took her name, which was quite common in the ancient world, from her native land. Apparently she was wealthy, because she sold expensive cloth. She offered her hospitality and material aid to Paul and his fellow travelers. The mission in Philippi was very successful and a Christian community soon formed, to whom later Paul would write the Epistle to the Philippians. This community was especially dear to Paul's heart, and he, even though he usually financially supported himself with manual labor, accepted money from this community for his needs during his travels several times, as well as during his imprisonment in Rome (Phil 1:5, 2:12, 4:14–16). A few of Paul's converts in Macedonia are even known by name: two women—Euodia and Syntyche—and two men—Epaphroditus and Clement (Phil 4:2, 3; 2:25).

Philippi turned out to be the first European city in which the apostles would be persecuted by pagans alone. The reason for this persecution was the exorcism, by St Paul, of an evil spirit from a certain slave girl who was able to foretell the future thanks to the demon inside her. This was a source of great revenue for her masters. After Paul exorcised the demon, the slave girl lost her ability to tell the future. This slave was apparently a kind of ventriloquist (i.e., she was able to force her voice to sound like it was coming from her stomach, suggested by the use of the Greek word *pithon*). As a result, the people considered her to be inspired by one of the gods, and many turned to her with petitions.

Paul and Silas Imprisoned, Their Miraculous Deliverance, and the Conversion of the Prison Guard (16:19–40).

When she encountered the preachers, the slave girl cried out, "These men are the servants of the Most High God, who proclaim to us the way of salvation." In these words we can see the unwilling confession of God's might even from a demon, something we have already encountered in the life of the Lord Jesus Christ. St John Chrysostom considers this confession to be ill intentioned. Paul became angry, not desiring to hear such a confession from the mouth of a demon. The Gospel, which destroys the work of the devil, has no need of his sanction. The masters of this slave, seeing that she had stopped prophesying, seized Paul and Silas and dragged them to the square where legal proceedings usually took place, to "the magistrates." These were the local Roman *duumviri*, the highest judicial magistrates in a city of the Roman Empire. They were elected *praetors* who were greatly honored and respected by the inhabitants of the city.

The masters of the slave girl accused the apostles as Jews who were disturbing the peace with the preaching of their religion (the word "customs" used by St Luke has a broad meaning, including all aspects of societal life, including religious and ecclesiastical ones). At this time in Rome, it was illegal to preach religions that contradicted the official pagan religion. It is also possible that the recent edict by Emperor Claudius concerning the expulsion of Jews from Rome (see Acts 18:2) had already come into effect. The masters of the slave girl managed to provoke the people of the city against the apostles as well. For this reason, the magistrates, without any juridical proceedings, had the apostles beaten with rods and imprisoned, keeping them under heavy guard. The night watchman placed them in an especially secure cell, "and fastened their feet in the stocks," to prevent any chance of escape.

But "the stricter the custody, the greater the miracle," in the words of St John Chrysostom[26]—Paul and Silas did not despair. On the contrary, filled with joy that they were counted worthy to suffer for the name of Christ, they began to pray loudly, singing psalms. Suddenly, a miraculous earthquake shook the prison to its foundations, and all the doors opened of their own accord. "Everyone's chains were loosed. And the keeper of the prison, awaking from sleep and seeing the prison doors open, supposing the prisoners had fled, drew his sword and was about to kill himself." Paul reassured him that all were still in their places. The guard asked for a torch and fell at the feet of Paul and Silas, acknowledging them as emissaries of God. Having led them into the outer part of the prison, where, apparently, the entire household of the keeper had gathered in fear, he asked them, "Sirs, what must I do to be saved?"

The miracle convinced him that these prisoners preached the only true path to salvation, and he expressed a desire to walk along this path, asking what was necessary to do so. The apostles required as a necessary condition that he believe in the Lord Jesus Christ and immediately catechized all present with the teaching Christ, after which the entire household was baptized. The prison warden took care of them. He washed and dressed their wounds; he invited them into his own home and fed them from his own table. The original Greek expression "brought them up" shows us that the jailer lived with his entire family in the upper story of the jail, while the prisoners were kept in the bottom stories. This also would explain why the entire household was awakened by the earthquake.

During the night, the magistrates most likely had a change of heart concerning their hasty punishment of Paul and Silas, and so, desiring to cover their fault and end the whole affair quietly, they sent officers to tell the jailer to free the prisoners. But Paul took advantage of his rights as a Roman citizen (Roman citizens were exempt from corporal punishment), and he required that the dishonor inflicted on Silas and him be publicly recanted, just as they had been publicly beaten. Of course, Paul did not do this for the sake of his wounded pride, but rather for the sake of the work that they did. If they had been released secretly from prison, then rumors could be spread that they had been imprisoned justly, and that they had escaped and had not been let go. This would have been damaging to the work of the mission. Therefore, Paul demanded a public justification by the magistrates.

Paul, a native of Tarsus, had Roman citizenship from birth (see Acts 22:18). It is possible that his father or another of his ancestors received the right of Roman citizenship for some service during Rome's wars. Or perhaps citizenship had been bought (see Acts 22:28). In any case, the magistrates were afraid when they found out Paul was a Roman citizen, because they themselves would be subject to punishment by illegally dishonoring a Roman citizen (if Paul and Silas were to file an official complaint). Therefore, the magistrates came and apologized in person, but asked Paul and Silas to leave the city quietly, fearing further disturbances. The apostles agreed, but first they came to Lydia to instruct the new community before parting. Because of the shift in perspective from first person plural back to the third person, it seems that Paul and Silas left alone, while Luke and Timothy remained for a time to help establish the new Christian community.

Acts Chapter Seventeen

Paul and Silas in Thessalonica (17:1–9) and in Berea (17:10–14). Paul in Athens and His Sermon in the Areopagus (17:15–34).

Paul and Silas in Thessalonica (17:1–9).

In four days, traveling along the military highway that stretched through Amphipolis and Apollonia, the preachers reached Thessalonica, the capital city of the second region of Macedonia (Amphipolis was the capital of the first region), located on the Thermaic Gulf of the Aegean Sea. This was a densely populated port city where the Roman praetor lived. Many Jews lived here as well, and there was a large synagogue. The Apostle Paul, as was customary for him, began preaching Christ first to the Jews. He attended the synagogue and disputed with the Jews during three consecutive Sabbath days, proving on the basis of Scripture that Jesus of Nazareth was the Messiah, Who was promised by the prophets, had to suffer and resurrect from the dead, and was foretold and promised in the Old Testament. This is the essence of all preaching of the Gospel and the Christian faith.

The result of these discussions was that some (apparently not many) of the ethnic Jews converted, while "a great multitude of the devout Greeks," that is, proselytes, "and not a few of the leading women, joined Paul and Silas." The Jews who did not believe—they were in the majority—were upset that so many proselytes and a few ethnic Jews were converted by these new preachers, and so they "took some of the evil men from the marketplace, and gathering a mob, set all the city in an uproar and attacked the house of Jason," who was apparently hosting the apostles. The mob wanted to lynch the apostles, but because they were not at home, they took Jason "and some brethren" to the city magistrates, accusing them of giving refuge to disturbers of the peace. The accusation was a political one, of course, because only such an accusation could have any chance of success. This tactic was used also by the high priests when trying to obtain Pilate's conviction of Christ: "These are all acting contrary to the decrees of Caesar, saying there is another king—Jesus."

Such a serious accusation troubled both the people and the magistrates, but since the accused were not actually present, the magistrates contented themselves with taking security from Jason (i.e., they held a deposit of money as a bond to encourage Jason to uphold the public peace in the future). Then they released everyone.

Paul and Silas in Berea (17:10–14).

When night came, the preachers departed to Berea, a city southwest of Thessalonica, in the third region of Macedonia, the capital of which was Pella. Berea was on the southern border of Macedonia. There, as usual, Paul went first to the synagogue. "These were more fair-minded than those in Thessalonica," less restricted by fanaticism and prejudice, and they accepted the preaching of the Gospel eagerly. In their spare time, they "searched the Scriptures daily to find out whether these things were so." The consequence of such conscientious searching of the Scriptures was that "many of them believed, and also not a few of the Greeks, prominent women as well as men." The Jews from Thessalonica, having found out that Paul was preaching in Berea, immediately came there and once again stirred up mobs from the rabble of the city. Then, the brethren immediately "sent Paul away, to go to the sea, but both Silas and Timothy remained there."

"So those who conducted Paul brought him to Athens." Doubtless, this was a journey by sea, for this was the easiest way of avoiding the Jews. Furthermore, if Paul had gone by land, his conscientiousness would not have allowed him to pass by all the cities along the way without first preaching in them (Acts tells of no other communities established between Berea and Athens). Timothy, who was left in Philippi, rejoined the apostles either in Berea or along the way. Paul now ordered Timothy and Silas both to come to him in Athens, but they only rejoined Paul in Corinth, probably because he left Athens rather quickly. In any case, reading 1 Thessalonians 2:18–3:2 makes it obvious that Timothy alone came to Paul in Athens, but Paul sent him back to Thessalonica, and only later, together with Silas who had remained in Berea, did he come to Paul in Corinth. From this passage in Thessalonians, we see that Paul tried twice to return to Thessalonica, but obstacles hindered him, and he sent Timothy from Athens instead.

Paul in Athens and His Sermon in the Areopagus (17:15–34).

While awaiting Silas and Timothy in Athens, Paul's "spirit was provoked within him when he saw that the city was given over to idols." Athens was the center of Greek religion, art, and riches; therefore, it was full of temples, altars, and statues to many different gods. The opulence of the architecture and statuary was legendary. This sort of external beauty always impresses people who value only physical, earthly beauty and refinement. But all this upset the moral fiber of the great apostle tremendously, because he saw underneath all the refinement to the darkness and perversion of human nature to which paganism led. As usual, he began to preach in the local synagogue, and in addition, he daily spoke and disputed with people he would meet in the squares or under the covered galleries.

Among these people were philosophers, people who loved to argue for the sake of argument. St Luke explicitly mentions the Stoics and Epicureans because these were the most popular philosophical schools, because their doctrines were more accessible to the masses than the doctrines of other schools. Moreover, it was the Epicureans and Stoics specifically who began to argue with Paul, probably because these philosophical systems were especially opposed to Christianity. Epicureanism was founded on crude materialism and nihilism, while the foundation of Stoicism was self-obsessed pride.

There seemed to be two opinions concerning Paul after these disputations. Some, probably the Epicureans, thought that Paul's words were empty babble. Others, probably the Stoics, were interested that the foreigner preached unknown gods, because Paul preached both Jesus Christ and the resurrection (*anastasis* in Greek), which (according to Chrysostom) they understood to be a separate deity. These Stoics, at the very least, did not reject Paul's words completely and desired to hear more, even if they found his words to be strange. They brought him—not by force, but by invitation—to the Areopagus, a place near the Acropolis that functioned as the high court of appeals for both criminal and civil cases. In pre-Classical times, it was the place where the council of elders of Athens would meet, a body similar to the Roman Senate. This council of elders continued to be respected even in Roman times. It was located on Mars Hill, adjacent to a large plaza, north of the western fortifications of the Acropolis. Paul was not brought here to be judged, however, but only to present his teaching to the representatives of the city's cultural and educated elite.

Standing in the midst of the Areopagus, Paul uttered a sermon that is the greatest model of both his apostolic wisdom and his rule to be as a pagan for the pagans, the better for them to hear the Gospel (see 1 Cor 9:19–22). Before his gaze stood the Acropolis with its complete collection of famous works of art; below him was the majestic Temple of Hephaestus; and all around him were many temples, altars, and statues of countless divinities—and all this was done with the skill of the best artists in the world. This was all fodder for Paul's introduction.

He praised the Athenians for their godliness. Notably, Paul here used a word that in Greek means both "piety" and "superstition" in the sense of base fear before an object of worship. Without offending the hearing of his listening, but at the same time not sacrificing the truth, Paul wisely chose this word that so well characterized the piety of the Athenians as pagan superstition. Even secular Greek writers witnessed that Athens had an altar to an unknown god. The explanation was simple: polytheism can never be sure that it honors all the gods. The fear that some unknown—and, therefore, unworshiped—divinities could become angry at this neglect inspired altars to be raised to these unknown gods to pacify them.

At the same time, doubtless this worship of the "unknown god" was an unwitting striving of polytheism toward the truth, an admission of its own worthlessness, and a search for the true God. This was the truth—only dimly glimpsed—that

Paul considered necessary to illuminate fully. "Therefore, the One whom you worship without knowing, Him I proclaim to you."

The following thoughts are then developed:

1. There is one God, the Creator of the universe.
2. He is completely independent of the material world.
3. All people were created, by the will of this God, from "one blood." Consequently, they have one and the same God. This is an important point, for ethnic differences were an important justification for regional polytheism.
4. The division of mankind into nations separated by place and time is willed by God's providence. All people must come to knowledge of God. This is their fate—to be led by God to knowledge of God.
5. This knowledge of God is not difficult, for God is not far from each of us. Something in the very nature of man unites him with God. Even the pagan poets spoke of this: "For we are also His offspring." Here Paul cited the *Phaenomena* of Aratus of Cilicia, an extremely popular poet who lived in the third century B.C. A similar phrase can also be found in a hymn by Cleanthes, the disciple of Zeno, to Zeus ("we are your generation").
6. Only a lamentable delusion of the mind can lead people to liken divinity to works of art, to things made with the hands.
7. Paul concludes his speech with a call to repentance, motivated by the coming judgment over the cosmos, "because He has appointed a day on which He will judge the world in righteousness by the Man Whom He has ordained," that is, Jesus Christ, Whom He raised from the dead.

Paul had hardly enough time to even name Jesus Christ, when some of the listeners, hearing of the resurrection from the dead, began to ridicule him, while others said, "We will hear you again on this matter." Most likely it was the Epicureans who mocked Paul, because their philosophy absolutely rejected the idea of the resurrection of the dead. Others were more respectful, but if these truly had a desire to "hear him again," Paul would have remained longer in Athens, but he left Athens very soon afterward. Forced to end his sermon in the middle, "Paul departed from among them." However, the wise words of Paul bore fruit. "Some men joined him and believed," among them Dionysius the Areopagite (i.e., a member of the Areopagus) and a woman named Damaris (tradition calls her the wife of Dionysius).

Dionysius, according to tradition, became a dedicated disciple of Paul and later was consecrated bishop of Athens. He preached in Gaul and was martyred in Paris. His memory is celebrated on October 3.

Thus, the harvest of Paul's wise sermon was not great, despite the great civilization of this most cultured of cities. Thus, "the world through wisdom did not know God" (1 Cor 1:21).

Acts Chapter Eighteen

Paul in Corinth (18:1–17). Paul Sails to Jerusalem Through Ephesus (18:18–23). The Beginning of His Third Missionary Journey (18:22–23). The Preaching of Apollos (18:24–28).

Paul in Corinth (18:1–17).

Having left Athens, Paul came to Corinth. This prosperous city, famous in ancient times for its trade, lay on an isthmus between the Aegean and Ionian Seas. It had two harbors—one on the western and one on the eastern edge of the city—and was at that time the capital of the Roman province of Achaia, which included the Peloponnesus and Hellas, that is, nearly all of today's Greece. Its inhabitants were known for their love of luxury and physical pleasures. Desiring to settle for a long time in Corinth, because it was an important central point for his mission, Paul began to support himself with manual labor while accepting the hospitality of a certain Aquila, a Pontian Jew who recently moved from Italy with his wife Priscilla. Both of them were tentmakers, as was Paul by trade.

Here is the first explicit reference to Claudius's expulsion of the Jews from Rome, something that is witnessed in Suetonius's histories. Suetonius writes that the reason for this edict was a disturbance caused by a Messianic Jew, calling himself "Christ." Most likely, Suetonius simply did not understand the intricacies of this situation, because the cause was most likely a disturbance of the Jews against local Christians, of whom there was a considerable number by this time. However, Suetonius's witness is still important, because it mentions Christ and because it helps us establish a clear chronology for the Book of Acts. Claudius's edict was issued in A.D. 52.

Both Aquila and Priscilla were converted to Christ by Paul, but probably a little later, for initially he stayed with them only "because he was of the same trade." It was customary for the Jews—even among the rich—to teach some trade to their children to make them financially independent. Tent making—travelers and armies alike used tents—was a lucrative trade. Paul mentions several times in his epistles that he was grateful that he had a way to support himself, thereby never becoming a burden on anyone (e.g., 1 Cor 4:12).

Every Sabbath, Paul preached in the synagogue, persuading both ethnic Jews and proselytes of the truth of the Gospel's teaching. Evidently, Paul encountered significant opposition, for he "was compelled by the Spirit," an expression indicating great spiritual strain. The opposition of the Jews was so great that they even openly blasphemed in the synagogue. Then Paul ceased all communication with the Corinthian synagogue and turned to the pagans of Corinth. "He shook his garments," something that is symbolically equivalent to shaking the dust off his feet, a sign of a complete and inexorable break, and said, "Your blood be upon your own heads; I am clean. From now on I will go to the Gentiles." In other words, for your unbelief and recalcitrance, terrible calamities will fall on your head as punishment from God, but I am not responsible for that. I preached the only possible way for you to avoid these punishments—the path of evangelical truth—but you did not listen to me. You are at fault and responsible, not I.

The punishment that Paul threatened here is eternal perdition, which is here referred to as eternal death (Rom 1:32; 6:16, 21, 23; 7:5, 10, 13); therefore, he used the image of flowing blood, as the soul of an animal is in its blood. Paul concluded his threat with the announcement that because they so stubbornly reject his preaching, he will now turn to the pagans. He fitted word to action immediately, and left the synagogue to move to the house of a proselyte named Justus, who lived near the synagogue. This categorical action was such a strong effect that many believed and were baptized, including the ruler of the synagogue, a man named Crispus, along with his entire household. Paul himself witnessed that he baptized Crispus in 1 Corinthians 1:14.

To encourage his faithful servant, the Lord Himself appeared to Paul in a vision during the night and said, "Do not be afraid, but speak, and do not keep silent." By this, the Lord indicated that in this city there were many people ready to hear Paul's preaching and convert. Paul—perhaps he was ready to abandon Corinth in frustration as he did Athens—remained there, preaching for a year and a half. In the meantime, the Jews did not want to leave him alone, even here. "When Gallio was proconsul," they attacked Paul and brought him before the judgment seat, accusing him of teaching people to worship God "contrary to the law."

Here, we can once again establish a clear historical chronology. The proconsul Lucius Junius Gallio Annaeanus, the brother of the famous Stoic philosopher Seneca (Nero's instructor) who, like Seneca, committed suicide during Nero's reign, was governor of Achaia from A.D. 53 to 54. According to Seneca, Gallio was a gentle man, modest and kind, and a talented administrator. All of these qualities are evident in St Luke's account. Gallio did not even wait to hear Paul's defense; as a political administrator, he considered the case to be beyond his jurisdiction, and he "drove them from the judgment seat," probably because they were causing a disturbance and did not want to leave. Incensed by the stubbornness of the Jews, the guards and other pagans who witnessed what occurred seized Sosthenes, the new ruler of the synagogue, and beat him right in front of the judgment seat. According to tradition, this Sosthenes also was converted by St Paul, was his fellow laborer in the faith (1 Cor 1:1), and later was the bishop of Colophon in Asia Minor.

Paul Sails to Jerusalem Through Ephesus (18:18–23).

From Corinth, Paul sailed to Syria along with Aquila and Priscilla. "He had his hair cut off at Cenchrea, for he had taken a vow." Cenchrea was the eastern harbor of Corinth, but the exact meaning of "he had his hair cut off" is not clear. There are many guesses, but most of them are not likely. This could not have been the Nazirite vow, because after the period of the vow, the Nazirite had to bring a lawful sacrifice, along with his hair, in the temple. This sacrifice could be brought only in Jerusalem. Likely, this was some kind of personal vow, but it is unclear what the reason for it was. Perhaps it had something to do with the dangers associated with Paul's journey, and this was Paul's way of giving thanks to God.

Having reached Ephesus, the capital of Ionia, which was a large city with plentiful trade—soon it would become the most important Christian center in Asia Minor—Paul left Aquila and Priscilla there and immediately went into the synagogue to preach. Apparently, he was received well, for they asked him to remain with them for a while longer. He promised to return to them, saying that he had to celebrate the coming feast in Jerusalem. He remained in Jerusalem not long, and then returned to Antioch, from where he planned to begin his third missionary journey.

The Beginning of His Third Missionary Journey (18:22–23).
Having spent some time in Antioch, Paul left on his third journey. He began by traveling through Galatia and Phrygia with the intention of strengthening his previously established communities in the faith. From a later chapter, it becomes obvious that he took Timothy and Erastus on this trip with him (19:22). Rather than continuing with Paul's journey, however, the writer of Acts makes an aside to tell of a certain Jew named Apollos, born in Alexandria, who was a powerful preacher of Christianity in Corinth (as we see in 1 Cor). St Luke speaks of him with praise as an eloquent man, well versed in Scripture.

The Preaching of Apollos (18:24–28).
Apollos probably came to Ephesus while Paul was journeying through Asia Minor on his third journey, and before Paul returned to Ephesus, Apollos traveled to Greece. He was instructed in the Christian faith, but not completely, because he only knew the baptism of John. Apparently, he himself was only baptized by the baptism of John, and so he did not have the gift of the Holy Spirit. Nevertheless, afire with ardent zeal, "he spoke and taught accurately the things of the Lord," though incompletely. When Aquila and Priscilla heard him in the Ephesian synagogue, they immediately noticed that he was not sufficiently instructed in the "way of God," and they invited him to their house and "took him aside and explained to him the way of God more accurately." It is likely that their instruction inspired his journey to Greece. His activity there, especially in Corinth, was powerful and fruitful. He ably proved to the Jews, on the basis of Scripture, that Jesus of Nazareth is truly the Messiah. Later, he became bishop of Smyrna before St Polycarp.

Acts Chapter Nineteen

The Apostle Paul's Third Missionary Journey. His Arrival in Ephesus and the Baptism of the Disciples of John (19:1–10). Paul's Miracles in Ephesus and Their Effect (19:11–20). Paul's Plans for Further Travels (19:21–22). Disturbance in Ephesus Against the Christians, Incited by Demetrius the Silversmith (19:23–40).

The Apostle Paul's Third Missionary Journey. His Arrival in Ephesus and the Baptism of the Disciples of John (19:1–10).
Traveling from Antioch to Ephesus was easiest by boat, but St Paul preferred the more difficult road through the mountainous regions of Asia Minor, because

he wanted to visit the churches he established. While Apollos was preaching in Corinth, Paul, having passed through Galatia and Phrygia, arrived in Ephesus. Ephesus was a free city within the empire, built on the banks of the river Cayster, between Miletene and Smyra, famous for its trade and its Temple of Artemis, as well as the fervency of the local cult of the "great goddess." At that time, it was the capital of proconsular Asia. The inhabitants of Ephesus were great lovers of physical pleasures and were enamored of magical practices. It was difficult to find in the entire empire a place more filled with fanaticism and superstition.

Paul's first visit to this city was of short duration, but the apostle returned there soon afterward and remained there for two years and a few months, much longer than he usually spent in any one place. The Church of Ephesus, established by Paul, later would become a famous Christian metropolia, giving the Church an entire series of famous bishops. Four hundred years later, Ephesus would be the place where the Third Ecumenical Council would denounce Nestorianism.

St Paul, supporting himself as before by making tents, could join with his fellow laborers from Corinth, whose home gradually became a place for the faithful to assemble (1 Cor 16:19). Here, Paul met with some disciples of John the Baptist, probably Jews who recently had moved to Ephesus. They kept company with the Christians, and Paul, noticing that they had incomplete knowledge of the ways of the Lord, learned that they were baptized only with the baptism of John, the preparatory baptism of repentance that did not have the power to grant the Holy Spirit. Therefore, he baptized them in the name of the Father, Son, and Holy Spirit, after which he laid hands on them and they were filled with the gracious gifts of the Holy Spirit. They immediately began to speak in tongues and prophesied. Altogether, there were about twelve disciples.

As usual, the first place of Paul's preaching was the local synagogue, where he fearlessly preached for three months. By this time, many among his listeners began to follow Christ, but as in all places, he encountered some who opposed him. Their opposition gradually became more virulent and hardened, until they began to blaspheme Christianity publicly. This forced Paul to break ties with the synagogue and the Jews definitively. Together with his newly converted disciples, he began to preach not only on Sabbath days, as in the synagogue, but every day in the school of a certain Tyrannus. Because this is a Greek name, we can assume that the school was a kind of hall where a pagan rhetorician taught philosophy. However, since the Jews of the Diaspora often had Greek or Roman names, it is also possible that this Tyrannus was a Jewish teacher who had a private synagogue or study hall in his home, called a *Beth Midrash*, where Jewish tradition and interpretations of Scripture were taught. We must assume that Tyrannus was positively disposed to Christianity, which is why he offered his study hall for Paul and his disciples.

Paul's Miracles in Ephesus and their Effect (19:11–20).

Paul preached in Ephesus for two years, and because it was such a large city, into which various people from all over Asia Minor constantly traveled either for trade or to worship Artemis, the "Diana of Ephesus," St Luke allowed himself the hyperbole of saying that "all who dwelt in Asia heard the word of the Lord Jesus." To strengthen the community, "God worked unusual miracles by the hands of Paul." Two are explicitly mentioned:

1. Various diseases were healed when the sick would merely touch an object that Paul used, such as a handkerchief or belt.
2. Demons were cast out of the possessed.

Interestingly, it was not Paul who performed the miracles of healing directly. Rather, others placed objects that he used on the sick, perhaps even without his knowledge, and still the sick were healed. It is an instructive example of how the miraculous power of God can act even through inanimate objects, something that Protestants refuse to believe, even though they claim to base the tenets of their faith on the word of God.

St Luke then says that Paul's glory became so great that some wandering Jewish magicians, of whom there were many at the time, began to emulate Paul. Some of these people who misused the name the Lord Jesus for their own purposes included the seven sons of the Jewish chief priest, Sceva. Who was this Sceva, and in what sense was he a "chief priest," is not clear. Perhaps, he was one of the temple priests, and his sons had left Judea to make money as traveling exorcists. But the evil spirit whom they tried to exorcise with the name of "Jesus whom Paul preaches" mocked them cruelly. It is wonderful that by his words—"Jesus I know, and Paul I know; but who are you?"—the demon admitted and even confessed the power and authority of the Lord Jesus Christ and Paul, while also despising these people who misused the name of Jesus. To prove to them how much he despised their misuse of power, the demon forced the man whom he possessed to attack the exorcists and beat them.

Rumors about this event spread far and wide in Ephesus, and all were filled with fear before this mystical, almighty power of the name of the Lord Jesus Christ. The people "magnified" this mighty name, by which such miracles were performed, and many, impressed greatly by this event, believed in Christ. Among them were those who practiced magic, and for the sake of their new faith in Christ, they "brought their books together," books that could have included magical formulas, books of spells, and prayers to various gods, "and burned them in the sight of all." As mentioned, Ephesus was a center of the cult of Artemis-Diana. "And they counted up the value of them, and it totaled fifty thousand pieces of silver."

Paul's Plans for Further Travels (19:21–22).

The great success of the Ephesian mission gave Paul good reason to leave and choose a new place to preach. He "purposed in the Spirit, when he had passed through Macedonia and Achaia, to go to Jerusalem, saying, 'After I have been there, I must also see Rome.'" This is the first indication of Paul's desire to visit the capital of the empire of the world. Later, the Lord more directly would show him the way to Rome (23:11), and he would arrive there, preach there, and during his second visit, he would receive his martyr's crown there. As we see in his words in Acts 24:17, the journey to Jerusalem through Macedonia and Achaia was intended as an aid mission to raise money for the churches in Palestine. He sent his fellow laborers Timothy and Erastus ahead of him, while he remained in Asia "for a time."

Disturbance in Ephesus Against the Christians, Incited by Demetrius the Silversmith (19:23–40).

Subsequent events, however, forced Paul to leave Ephesus and Asia sooner that he had intended. A certain silversmith named Demetrius raised a commotion against Paul. This silversmith made "no small profit" on reproductions of the Temple of Artemis sold to religious tourists. The cult of Artemis was widespread in Asia Minor, and her temple in Ephesus (destroyed by Herostratus on Alexander the Great's birthday) was rebuilt with such magnificence that it was considered to be one of the Seven Wonders of the World. These reproductions of the temple and small idols of Artemis herself were greatly coveted by the followers of the cult; they were placed in homes, taken as charms during difficult journeys, and so on. It is entirely natural that Demetrius's work was profitable. It is even likely that he ran something like a silversmith factory to make these figurines.

Having gathered all the artists and artisans in his pay, Demetrius spoke with great emotion about how Paul had harmed their work and their goddess by turning many people in Ephesus and Asia away from her worship. This speech, combining religious fervor with fear of economic loss, stirred up hatred of Paul. With the cry, "Great is Diana of the Ephesians!" the mob began to rampage through the entire city. Paul's companions Gaius and Aristarchus were seized and taken into "the theater," either to force the magistrates to bring judgment or merely to lynch them. Apparently, they did not find Paul and Silas.

Paul's great bravery and power of spirit impelled him to speak to the mob, but the Christians and even "some of the officials of Asia, who were his friends," convinced him not to do this, fearing for his life. The constantly growing mob loudly clamored in the theater, and confusion reigned, for many of the people did not really know what they were doing there. The Jews then pushed forward a certain Alexander to speak to the mob. It was not entirely clear whether he was going to speak for or against the Christians. It is possible that the Jews were afraid that they would suffer along with the Christians, because they were known as enemies of idols, and perhaps they wanted to justify themselves, leaving the mob's anger to fall on the Christians. But no sooner did the people find out that Alexander was a Jew than they refused to listen to him, shouting "Great is Diana of the Ephesians" for more than two hours straight.

Finally, the city clerk quieted the crowd and spoke to them with words full of wisdom. "What man is there who does not know that the city of the Ephesians is temple guardian of the great goddess Diana, and of the image which fell down from Zeus?" In other words, because this is indisputable fact, there is no reason to cause trouble in the streets. The two Macedonians they brought "are neither robbers of temples nor blasphemers of your goddess." He then reminded Demetrius and his followers that if they had a legitimate complaint, it should be brought before the authorities in the lawful manner. Otherwise, they ran the risk of being guilty of disturbing the peace. This was obviously a threat of Roman reprisal, which immediately worked. The crowd dispersed.

Acts Chapter Twenty

Paul's Journey to Macedonia and Greece and Back to Troas (20:1–6). Paul Raises Eutychus in Troas (20:7–12). Further Travels to Mytilene (20:13–17). Paul's Farewell Address to the Presbyters of Ephesus (20:18–38).

Paul's Journey to Macedonia and Greece and Back to Troas (20:1–6).

After some time had passed, Paul decided to end his stay in Asia. Having gathered the Ephesian Christians, he instructed them and said farewell. He then traveled to Macedonia and Greece. There he remained for three months, probably spending most of his time in Corinth, where he met Apollos for the first time. The Corinthian community was especially dear to Paul's heart. Certain problems in the community worried and grieved the apostle, but their spiritual growth and gifts gave him great joy as well (see 1 Cor 5:7; 12:4–11, 28). From Corinth, Paul wrote his Epistle to the Romans (Acts 19:21, compare with Rom 15:28). His plan, evidently, was to travel by sea to Palestine, but when he found out about a Jewish conspiracy to seize and kill him on the way to the port, he changed his plan. He departed by land on a road leading through Macedonia. Having arrived in Philippi, Paul sent Titus back to Corinth with his second Epistle to the Corinthians, which is remarkable for its warmth of feeling and gentle love for his flock.

From Philippi, he traveled to Troas, but contrary winds made the journey last an uncharacteristically long five days. Paul was accompanied by seven men—three were Macedonians and four were from Asia Minor. Sopater was from Berea, Aristarchus and Secundus were from Thessalonica, and Gaius was from Derbe in Lycaonia (not the same Gaius who was taken by Demetrius's mob, because that Gaius was a Macedonian). Timothy we already know, and Tychius and Trophimus were from Ephesus. They awaited Paul in Troas. Why they went ahead of Paul, St Luke does not say, but perhaps it was to arrange a ship for Paul to travel on from Troas, for the subsequent account suggests that Paul had a ship specially arranged for his personal use.

PAUL RAISES EUTYCHUS IN TROAS (20:7–12).

Paul and his fellow travelers remained in Troas for seven days. Since the departure was scheduled for the morning of Monday, the brethren of Troas gathered "on the first day of the week," that is, Sunday evening, "to break bread," that is, to partake of the Eucharist, after which would follow the agape meal in a well-lit upper room. Paul's discussion with his beloved disciples was lengthy; evidently, neither teacher nor students wanted to stop this last discussion. During this conversation, which lasted until midnight, a certain youth named Eutychus, who sat on a windowsill, fell asleep. Not that he was lazy, but he was simply exhausted, and as he fell asleep, he fell out of the open window three floors down and died from the impact. The Greek text makes it clear that this young man was not "like dead" (*hos nekros*), but actually dead (*nekros*). Everyone began to weep and make a great deal of noise. Paul came down and lay on the body of Eutychus (as Elijah did over the son of the Sareptan widow in 4 Kgdms 17:21 and as Elisha did in 4 Kgdms 4:34). He hugged him and said, "do not trouble yourselves" (in the Greek it is literally, "stop your wailing") "for his life is in him." This expression does not mean that the boy did not die. It meant that his soul had returned to his body, that he had been raised from the dead. But St Paul in his humility does not express himself so openly, in order not to excite the people's praise for such a great miracle.[27]

When they came back up to the upper room, broke bread, and ate, Paul continued to speak with them until the sun rose, and only then did he leave, not allowing himself to rest after such a long vigil. "And they brought the young man in alive, and they were not a little comforted," both by his being alive and by their teacher having performed such a great miracle.

FURTHER TRAVELS TO MITYLENE (20:13–17).

The Apostle Paul decided that he would be able to reach Assos on foot by himself, and his fellow travelers could travel by sea and meet him there. Assos was a coastal town in Misia, about ten miles south of Troas, opposite the island of Lesbos. It seems that Paul undertook this leg of the journey alone on foot; however, no reason is given for this. From Assos, they together traveled to Mitylene, the capital of Lesbos, located on the island's eastern side. After spending the night there, they sailed away and stopped opposite Chios. The next day they arrived in Samos and remained in Trogyllium, a coastal town not far from Ephesus, and on the following day, they arrived in Miletus, another coastal city about nine miles from Ephesus.

St Luke makes it explicitly clear why they avoided Ephesus: "so that he would not have to spend time in Asia, for he was hurrying to be at Jerusalem, if possible, on the Day of Pentecost." Obviously, if he had come to the large Christian community in Ephesus, he would have had to remain there some time. But although he did not enter Ephesus, he still desired to part with the elders of the Ephesian Church, and he called them to himself in Miletus. The leaders of the church of Ephesus, summoned by Paul, were called "presbyters" (literally "elders") in 20:17, whereas in 20:28, the apostle calls them "bishops" (literally "overseers").

Were these "presbyters" or "bishops"? Both of these titles were used in civil governments even before they were appropriated for ecclesiastical use. Neither in their etymology nor in their original use does anything suggest a difference in rank between a "presbyter" and a "bishop." Bishop, a term initially more in use among the Greeks, indicates a priestly office. The word presbyter, meaning a person of advanced years, was used more among the Jews, and indicates more the ecclesiastical dignity in general than a specific office. In the early Church, the meaning of these two words was still fluid; however, this does not mean that the calling of bishop did not differ from the calling of a presbyter in their later sense. In other words, they were neither interchangeable nor exactly synonymous. The Apostle Paul himself strictly differentiated them, as we see in his Epistles to Titus (1:5) and Timothy (5:19, 22), in which he gives only the bishop the power and right to ordain a presbyter and judge him.

Those whom Paul called to himself were doubtless presbyters, but since distinct orders of priesthood had not yet developed, Paul called them "bishops" (or "overseers"), by which he accurately described their responsibilities—to oversee the souls of those entrusted to them.

Paul's Farewell Address to the Presbyters of Ephesus (20:18–38).
When the elders of the Ephesian Church—according to St Irenaeus of Lyons, the elders of other Asian churches were present as well—had arrived, St Paul addressed them with a touching farewell that is especially important, because it contains precious counsel for pastors in general. In this speech, St Paul summarized the work that he had done in Ephesus; he foretold the fate awaiting him in Jerusalem; he encouraged pastors to be vigilant against heretics, and he committed all of them to God. This speech can be divided into four parts.

In the first part (20:18–21), the Apostle Paul reminded them how he bore himself among them for three years, how zealous he was for the spread of the word of God, "serving the Lord with all humility, with many tears and trials," how he constantly taught all—Jews and Greeks—to repent before God and to believe in the Lord Jesus Christ.

In the second part (20:22–27), he spoke about the immediate future and told of the trials that awaited him, as well as his readiness to endure them with self-rejection and even joy. He was intent on Jerusalem, "bound in the spirit," although he knew what sorrows and even bonds awaited him there, since "the Holy Spirit testifies in every city"—probably through local prophets, such as Agabus, who would prophecy his bonds just in the next chapter—"saying that chains and tribulations await me." He was ready for all this and did not even "count his life dear." All he hoped was for the Lord to allow him to continue his apostolic calling to the very end. Sensing that he would no longer see his beloved Ephesians, Paul announced that his conscience was clear concerning his actions among them, because he never missed an opportunity to tell them of the will of God in full ("I am innocent of the blood of all men" means that he is not guilty of anyone's eternal perdition).

In the third part (20:28–31), Paul gave them pastoral counsel. "Therefore take heed to yourselves and to all the flock, among which the Holy Spirit has made you overseers, to shepherd the church of God which He purchased with His own blood." I am guiltless of the blood of any man, and so you should strive to be as well, and for this you should be vigilant to your own selves as well as to the state of your flock: "therefore, be vigilant." As Blessed Theophylact said, "when we take heed to ourselves, then the flock receives benefit."[28] It is not men who appointed you to your calling, but the Holy Spirit through the laying on of hands (Acts 14:23) to oversee the welfare of the Church, just as shepherds watch over their sheep. This spiritual flock entrusted to you is especially precious and requires especial vigilance and care, because they were bought with the precious Blood of Christ, through the death on the Cross, the atoning sacrifice for the sins of all mankind.

This vigilance is especially necessary because Paul could foresee the imminent coming of "savage wolves ... not sparing the flock," that is, false teachers or heretics. The Apostle Paul indicated two types of such false teachers. Some would enter the Church of Ephesus from the outside; some would arise from within their midst. Ephesus was one of the cultural centers of Asia Minor, where the religious and philosophical systems of both East and West came into contact; therefore, it was logical to expect heresies to arise in this city rather than in some other.

When the apostle, three years later, wrote an Epistle to the Ephesians from his Roman imprisonment, the false teachers had not yet reached Ephesus, but heresies already had arisen in the Phrygian city of Colossae. We know this also from the Epistle to the Colossians, written at the same time. From Paul's Epistles to Timothy (written later), then bishop of Ephesus, we see that similar heretics had arrived in Ephesus by that time. These are the same heretics against whom the apocalyptic letters and First General Epistle of St John the Theologian and the Epistle of Jude were directed. As an example of vigilance, Paul offered the Ephesians himself, reminding them how he "for three years ... did not cease to warn everyone night and day with tears." (Three years is not an exact figure, of course, but rather a "rounding up" of the three months of teaching in the synagogue and two years of teaching in the school of Tyrannus.)

In the fourth part of his speech (20:32–35), Paul blessed them, committing them to God and "to the word of His grace," encouraging them to follow his example of nonacquisitiveness, according to the words of the Lord: "it is more blessed to give than to receive."[29] Why did the Apostle Paul desire to live by the profit of his own labor, when he clearly instructed (following the words of the Lord Jesus Christ) that every laborer be worthy of his hire (Matt 10:10) and that the preachers of the Gospel must live on the benefaction of others (1 Cor 9:7–11, 13–14)? In answer, one must say that Paul never refused to accept whatever money was given to him (see Acts 16:15; 2 Cor 11:8), but he tried not to ask anything, lest money become a hindrance to his preaching, for converted pagans were not yet comfortable with financially supporting their pastors. He could have been chary of laying such a burden on them too early, lest the enemies of Christ's faith took advantage of this to slander Paul, calling him an avaricious man, personally profiting from the new faith. At the same time, he considered it an honor to serve the Church with his own means, and he never demanded anything of anyone, other than that they revere God and save their souls (1 Cor 9:16–18, 2 Cor 12:14, Thess 2:9). Furthermore, he wanted to give his disciples an example of the spiritual benefits of a poor and hardworking life.

Interestingly, the quote that Paul attributed to Christ is not found anywhere in the Gospels or any other God-inspired books. It is likely that this was a quote preserved in oral tradition as genuine words of Christ. This thought, of course, does not say that taking is an evil deed; however, to give to others is doubtless better than to take for oneself.

In conclusion, the Apostle Paul bowed to his knees and prayed together with all of them. They parted with him, greatly grieved and upset, because he declared to them that he would never see them again. Then they accompanied him to the ship.

Acts Chapter Twenty-One

Paul's Journey from Miletus to Caesaria (21:1–9). Paul in Caesaria and the Prophecy of His Imminent Bonds (21:10–14). Paul's Arrival in Jerusalem; the Jews Cause a Disturbance Against Him, and He Is Imprisoned (21:15–40).

Paul's Journey from Miletus to Caesaria (21:1–9).

Having sailed away from Miletus with a good wind, the travelers "running a straight course" came to Cos, a small island in the Aegean Sea known for its wines and production of expensive fabrics, located southwest of Miletus. From there, they reached Rhodes, a large island fifteen miles to the southeast, and then they arrived in Patara, a large coastal trade town in Lycia, a province of Asia Minor that had a famous Oracle of Apollo. From Troas to Patara, St Paul and his fellow travelers sailed on one ship, which, judging by certain actions he took (Acts 20:13, 16), was probably hired exclusively for his use. In Patara, they took passenger berths on a trading vessel bound for Phoenicia. The ship entered open sea, going toward Cyprus, which it passed on the left, so that by the end of the week, they cast anchor in the harbor of Tyre, where the trading goods were scheduled to be unloaded.

In Tyre, Paul and his fellow travelers met with local Christians. They remained seven days with them, after which they traveled to Jerusalem, although the brethren of Tyre, to whom Paul's fate was revealed by the Holy Spirit, asked him not to go to Jerusalem. However, Paul, as he himself said, was "bound by the Spirit" to follow through with his journey, and he could not listen to them, although they spoke out of love for him. Together with their wives and children, the brethren accompanied Paul to the shore, where they parted with him after praying together. The travelers again took a ship, not to be held up by a journey over land, and arrived in Ptolemais, the ancient coastal town of Akko, located south of Phoenicia, within Palestine proper. According to the ancient divisions, this land belonged to the tribe of Asher, a bit north of Mt Carmel. There they stayed a day with the local Christian community. On the next day, they continued their journey on foot along the beautiful Plain of Sharon toward Caesaria.

Paul in Caesaria and the Prophecy of His Imminent Bonds (21:10–14). After a day on foot, they arrived in Caesaria at the home of one of the seven deacons, Philip, known as "the Evangelist" for his zealous preaching of the Gospel. His amazing gifts were also present in his children—four of his daughters prophesied. Here, Paul received the last warning of his coming tribulations. A certain prophet named Agabus came from Judea (this was the same Agabus who foretold a famine in Judea, which caused the Antiochian Church to send Barnabas and Saul to Judea with aid). With a vivid symbolic gesture, Agabus took Paul's own belt and tied his own hands and feet. He then prophesied that the Jews would bind Paul in Jerusalem in the same way, before delivering him to the pagans. Paul's fellow travelers and the Caesarian Christians begged Paul not to go to Jerusalem, but Paul, submitting to the Spirit (though he was moved by the tears of the Christians) remained firm in his intention, saying not only that he wished to be bound but also that he was even ready to die for the name of the Lord Jesus in the same Jerusalem where he had persecuted the confessors of that name, and where the Lord Himself suffered and died.

Such loyalty to the will of God calmed everyone, and they also decided to submit to the will of God, saying, "The will of the Lord be done." Having prepared everything for the journey and the coming feast of Pentecost in Jerusalem, they traveled to the holy city. Some of the Caesarian Christians accompanied them to lead the apostle and his fellow travelers to the house of "a certain Mnason of Cyprus, an early disciple, with whom they were to lodge." Judging by his Greek name, Mnason was either a pagan convert or a former proselyte. He showed Paul great hospitality. It is likely that Paul was placed in his house so that the news of his arrival would not immediately reach the Jews, and so that they would not immediately be able to find him.

Paul's Arrival in Jerusalem; the Jews Cause a Disturbance Against Him, and He Is Imprisoned (21:15–40).

On the next day, the Apostle Paul and his fellow travelers came to the Apostle James, the bishop of Jerusalem, where all the local presbyters also gathered. No other apostles are here mentioned; apparently, they were preaching in other countries. Having greeted the triumphant assembly gathered in honor of his arrival, the Apostle Paul probably immediately passed on the aid he had gathered for the Church in Jerusalem among the Gentiles, an expression of brotherly love and the communion of churches. Then he told them in detail of God's work in founding the Church among the pagans.

Having heard him, the assembly glorified God, but they did not hide from him that the Christian communities of converted Jews, all extremely zealous for the Mosaic Law, were prejudiced against him, a prejudice founded on false rumors that Paul was trying to pervert the Jews of the Diaspora by preaching the cancelation of circumcision and all other ritual observances of the Mosaic Law. Evidently, these rumors were spread by the same opponents of Paul who were disturbing the Church in Antioch and Jerusalem with their requirements that even Gentiles be circumcised before baptism and that they be subject to all the rites of the Law of Moses.

Obviously, this accusation was entirely false. In all of his teaching, revealed especially in his epistles, Paul taught that salvation in Christ is not contingent on circumcision and following the Law of Moses, but only on faith in Christ. The most important condition for salvation is faith, while the works of the Law are not essential for a Christian. One may follow them if one wishes, but one should not hope to be saved by the observance of the Law. We saw that the Apostle Paul himself circumcised Timothy; consequently, one cannot paint him as an enemy of the Law of Moses, as his opponents tried to do. To destroy this prejudice against Paul and to uncover the lies of his opponents, the presbyters of Jerusalem counseled Paul to make a universal display of his respect for the Law of Moses by undergoing purification rites with four other people who had taken an oath and by paying "their expenses so that they may shave their heads" and bring the lawful sacrifice at the conclusion of their oath. By joining these four people and giving the same oath, and by paying for them, Paul would be performing a good deed that would vividly prove all the accusations false.

This shaving of the head was the culmination of a temporary Nazirite oath (not a lifelong one), consonant with Numbers 6. From this we see that Jewish Christians still performed the rites of the Mosaic Law, for in verse 23, the presbyters said, "*We* have four men." At the same time, the presbyters reminded Paul that the decision of the Apostolic Council concerning the rules for converted Gentiles remained in full force, and their counsel merely was offered in prudence, a concession to the weaknesses of the Jewish brethren. This counsel in no way contradicted

Paul's own teachings, and so he agreed. Having joined with the four Nazirites, he did everything required of him by the Law, having announced to the priest in the temple of his participation in the fulfillment of the oath and of his desire to pay for the offerings of all five at the conclusion of the seven days of purification.

The seven days had not even finished when a riot erupted against Paul, leading to his imprisonment. The Jews from Asia—that is, Ephesus and the surrounding areas—saw Paul in the temple. Evidently, they were there for the feast of Pentecost, and they were filled with hatred at the sight of Paul, but their hatred also was tinged with joy that they would now have a convenient opportunity to harm their enemy, hoping even to kill Paul. Truly they were able to stir up "the whole crowd" with their cries that "this is the man who teaches all men everywhere against the people, the law, and this place." The reason for the last accusation was that they saw Paul speaking with a certain Trophimus the Ephesian, and assumed that he had brought him into the temple, defiling it (pagans were forbidden from entering the Court of Israel).

If their first accusation was nothing but slander, based at least partly on a misunderstanding or confusion, the second accusation was clearly a fabrication, in which a false suspicion was uttered as indisputable truth. Because of the gravity of the accusations, "all the city was disturbed." A mob seized Paul and threw him out of the Court of Israel, and immediately locked the doors, lest the holy place be defiled by their planned lynching. Never was St Paul in a more dangerous situation. But in this moment, when all hope for deliverance seemed lost, unexpected aid appeared. Claudius Lysias, the local Roman commander overseeing the troops garrisoned near the so-called Tower of Antonia, which overlooked the temple from the northwest, was informed of a disturbance in the city. Immediately, he hurried to the place with his troops, and the mob, afraid of bloody reprisal, stopped beating Paul.

When Lysias saw who was the cause of the disturbance, he approached Paul and commanded him to be chained. He began to ask him who he was and what he had done. Because of the commotion—some were shouting one thing, others another—he could find out nothing for sure, and so he commanded Paul to be taken into the barracks. This was not easily done because of the size of the mob that loudly demanded Paul's death, so that even as they approached the steps leading to the garrison, the soldiers had to carry Paul.

Before the doors to the garrison closed, Paul desired to speak to the people who had only just before so unfairly attacked him, and he asked permission of the commander. He spoke to Lysias in Greek, which surprised him and showed his initial impression of Paul—that he was an Egyptian who recently had stirred up a rebellion—to be incorrect (evidently Lysias knew for a fact that the Egyptian could not speak Greek). This Egyptian was a magician who styled himself as a prophet and had many followers among the Zealots (sicarii or "dagger-bearers").

This fanatic brought his followers from the Judean desert to the Mount of Olives, convincing them that the walls of Jerusalem would fall before them as the walls of Jericho had fallen a long time ago. He also promised them the overthrow of the Romans and the beginning of the kingdom of the Messiah. Felix, the procurator, dispersed this horde, killing four hundred and taking another two hundred into captivity. However, the Egyptian himself managed to escape.

As we said before, Lysias initially believed Paul to be this Egyptian trying to raise a new force, but from Paul's knowledge of Greek, he realized his error. Paul explained that he was born in the well-known Cilician city of Tarsus, although he was a pure-blooded Jew. He asked permission to address the mob. Lysias gave his permission, and Paul, making a sign with his hand for silence, began to speak from the stairs overlooking the mob in "the Hebrew language," that is, in the Aramaic dialect used as a conversational language among the Jews at that time.

Acts Chapter Twenty-Two

The Apostle Paul Speaks to the Crowd About His Conversion and His Calling to the Apostolic Ministry (22:1–21). The Cries of the Mob, the Order to Beat Paul, and the Cancellation of That Order (22:22–29). Paul Before the Sanhedrin (22:30).

The Apostle Paul Speaks to the Crowd About His Conversion and His Calling to the Apostolic Ministry (22:1–21).

"Brethren and fathers," began Paul. "Brethren" was intended for all those present, while "fathers" was a respectful address to those in authority and those of advanced years. "Hear my defense before you now," the defense referring to the false accusations of the Asian Jews. When they heard that he was speaking in Hebrew, the silence deepened. Paul then gave a detailed account of his nationality and his education, hoping to show everyone that he was truly a Jew and a zealot of the Law. He told them that he was raised in the full strictness of the Mosaic Law "at the feet of Gamaliel" and that he persecuted Christians "to the death"—meaning with as much force as he was capable of—something that the high priest himself could witness, as well as the council of elders.

Then Paul told them of his conversion to Christ on the road to Damascus. This account is completely consonant with Acts 9:3–8. There are only a few extra details in this version that Paul underlined here. He mentioned that the bright light of the Lord's presence covered him "about noon," which is obviously an unusual and miraculous phenomenon. He also mentioned that the Lord called Himself not simply "Jesus," but "Jesus of Nazareth," that "those who were with [him] indeed saw the light and were afraid, but they did not hear the voice of Him who spoke." Consequently, this event was not a delusion, not a personal hallucination of Paul's. His fellow travelers' not hearing the voice does not contradict Acts 9, for we must understand Paul's words to mean that they heard a voice but did not understand the words.

From these two accounts, we can reconstruct a full picture. The revelation was given exclusively to Paul, while his fellow travelers saw and heard only, so to speak, the reverberation or echo of this revelation. Then, St Paul told of his blindness and healing and baptism at the hand of Ananias, and he underlined that Ananias was "a devout man according to the Law, having a good testimony with all the Jews who dwelt [in Damascus]." That is, this was not some unknown person, but a man generally accepted as a follower of the Law.

To the account of his conversion, Paul added an account of the Lord's appearance to him in Jerusalem, which St Luke does not mention in the previous account, nor does Paul mention in any other speech or epistle. This vision occurred when Paul returned to Jerusalem, having spent a long time in Arabia, where he traveled after his conversion in Damascus. Paul makes a special point to underline that this vision occurred in the temple during prayer; consequently, even after his conversion, he did not cease to pray and worship lawfully in the temple. St Paul also underlined that he was not an enemy of the Jewish nation, for when the Lord commanded him to leave Jerusalem, Paul himself argued with God, desiring to preach in the place where he previously persecuted the Christians. Only Jesus's second, insistent command forced Paul to leave Jerusalem.

The Cries of the Mob, the Order to Beat Paul, and the Cancellation of That Order (22:22–29). Paul Before the Sanhedrin (22:30).

Until this moment, the Jews calmly listened; however, when Paul said that the Lord told him to "depart, for I will send you far from here to the Gentiles," they began to scream in fanatical zeal, causing the mob to explode in anger, because they considered Paul to have only confirmed the accusations leveled at him. In a wild expression of their fanaticism and anger they "tore off their clothes and threw dust into the air," as though readying to stone him. Not understanding what was happening, and fearing that the truth would not come out because of the mob's commotion, Lysias commanded Paul to be taken into the Tower of Antonia and beaten, thinking to use torture to find out the whole truth of Paul's alleged crime.

When Paul was already tied to the whipping post, he calmly explained Lysias's twofold infraction of Roman Law concerning citizens: (1) As a Roman citizen, Paul was exempt from corporal punishment, as this was a punishment for slaves; and (2) It was an infraction against Roman criminal law for a tribute to begin criminal proceedings against a defendant with torture.

Paul's admission of Roman citizenship worried the centurion who was assigned to oversee the beating, and he immediately told Lysias. Lysias himself had spent a great deal of money to acquire Roman citizenship, and he doubted this poor preacher could have afforded such a luxury. Having found out that Paul was a citizen from birth, however, he believed him and was afraid, not only because he had commanded to have him beaten, but also because he had him chained without a trial, for the chaining of a Roman citizen without an initial investigation into his culpability was considered a crime in itself, punishable by Roman Law.

Because Lysias still knew nothing concrete about Paul's guilt, or even what his alleged crime was, he commanded that the Sanhedrin meet to officially charge Paul and determine his guilt or innocence. However, Lysias did not immediately take the chains off Paul, but only on the next day, most likely because he was stubborn. Then, having led Paul out, he brought him before the Sanhedrin in the usual place of its session, probably in one of the wings of the temple.

Acts Chapter Twenty-Three

The Apostle Paul Before the Sanhedrin and the Dissension Among His Accusers (23:1–10). *The Vision of the Lord Jesus* (23:11). *A Conspiracy to Murder Paul* (23:12–22). *Paul Is Sent to Caesaria to the Procurator Felix* (23:23–35).

The Apostle Paul Before the Sanhedrin and the Dissension Among His Accusers (23:1–10).

As did Christ Himself and the elder Apostles before him, Paul now stood before the supreme council of the Jewish nation. "Looking earnestly at the council," his gaze firm and calm, he began his speech with apostolic dignity, not even waiting to be questioned by the Sanhedrin, because it was not they who called him to be judged, but the Roman authority that had brought him before them. "Men and brethren," he said, "I have lived in all good conscience before God until this day." In acknowledgment of his own innocence and his apostolic ministry, he denied these unlawful judges their honorific title of "fathers" or "leaders of the people" and insisted on the purity of his conscience in his doing of God's work.

These words of the apostle seemed hypocritical or self-serving to the high priest Ananias, and he commanded Paul to be struck on the mouth. This Ananias, a proud and hard man, was the acting high priest at the time (not one of the several in attendance who had the title "high priest" merely as an honorific), the son of Nebedeus, preceded by Josephus ben Camydus and succeeded by Ishmael ben Fabus. He was later sent to Rome for trial, but Claudius acquitted him, and he remained high priest until Felix removed him from his post in A.D. 52.

Paul, filled with righteous indignation, uttered harsh words against Ananias: "God will strike you, you whitewashed wall!" Ananias's command insulted God's Law, the truth, and the purity of Paul's own conscience. These words were not only a reproach for the unlawful command of the unjust judge, who had to judge by the Law, but a prophecy as well. After a few years, in the beginning of the Jewish Wars, Ananias was killed by the *sicarii* as a traitor. "Whitewashed wall" is an expression indicating hypocrisy and is synonymous with "whitewashed tomb" (Matt 23:27).

All those assembled considered Paul's words to be an insult to the high priest, a crime as serious as insulting God Himself. "I did not know, brethren, that he was the high priest," Paul said. Several interpretations have been offered for these words, but we need not consider any other than the literal one offered by St John Chrysostom. The Apostle Paul truly did not know that this was the high priest, for the high priests were changed regularly at that time, and one could not distinguish the acting high priest from other members of the Sanhedrin by their clothes alone. It was not always necessarily the high priest who presided at meetings of the Sanhedrin: the Sanhedrin had the right to choose a chairman for each meeting separately, and the Apostle Paul could not assume that the chairman of this session was the acting high priest, as this session was called in a demeaning fashion by the Roman authority.

Having seen that this was a lawless assembly that was prejudiced against him from the start, Paul decided a formal defense of his innocence would be inappropriate, because no one was likely to consider it anyway. So the holy apostle, with the wondrous support of the Holy Spirit, decided with perspicacity and wisdom on a single course of action, which always was effective in any situation in which one's listeners already were irritated and disturbed in thought. He took advantage of the fact that the Sanhedrin consisted of two opposite parties that were irremediably antagonistic toward each other—the Pharisees and Sadducees.

Having in mind that the Sadducees rejected the resurrection from the dead, as well as the existence of angels and the souls of the dead, while the Pharisees insisted on the existence of both, Paul loudly exclaimed: "Men and brethren, I am a Pharisee, the son of a Pharisee; concerning the hope and resurrection of the dead I am being judged!" By doing this, Paul effectively blocked—at least for a time—the unified action of the Sanhedrin and inclined the Pharisees to his cause. By saying these words, Paul underlined that he was being unjustly judged as a breaker and enemy of the Law of Moses, because he belonged to the party most zealous for the Law. He was not a traitor to Moses, as were the Sadducees, for example, who denied some of the truths of the Law of Moses. As for the teaching concerning the resurrection from the dead, Christian teaching agreed completely with the Pharisees, and thus, it was closer to it than the heresy of the Sadducees, who sinned against such an important dogmatic truth. The words of the apostle had their intended result, immediately leading to angry dissension and division in the Sanhedrin. The scribes of the party of the Pharisees even went so far as to place Paul under their protection, repeating the words of the Gamaliel: "let us not fight against God."

Both sides argued so loudly and the commotion was so great—some defended Paul, others attacked him—that Lysias became afraid that Paul might become a victim of their mutual recriminations. He did not want them to tear Paul, a Roman citizen, apart, for which he would have had to answer personally. Therefore, he commanded the soldiers to come from the barracks to the place of the Sanhedrin's session (perhaps in the Court of the Gentiles, where the pagan soldiers could enter without defiling the temple) and take Paul back to the Tower of Antonia.

The Appearance of the Lord Jesus to St Paul (23:11).

In this difficult position, the Lord encouraged his faithful apostle by appearing to him the next night, either in a vision or in a dream (it is not clear from the text which it was), and said, "Be of good cheer, Paul; for as you have testified for Me in Jerusalem, so you must also bear witness at Rome." By these words, the Lord calmed Paul, assuring him that the Jews were in no state to do anything evil to him, because he was called to preach in the very center of the Greco-Roman world—the political capital of the great Roman Empire. This greatly consoled Paul, because it also corresponded with his own desire to visit Rome and preach there.

A Conspiracy to Murder Paul (23:12–22).

In the meantime, the danger only increased for Paul. More than forty Jews who especially hated Paul—likely they were some of the Asian Jews, aided and abetted by the local Sadducees—bound themselves with a terrible oath: not to "eat nor drink till they had killed Paul." They made the members of the Sanhedrin complicit in their conspiracy by asking them to make a formal request of the Roman commander to bring Paul once more before the Sanhedrin to be judged. They intended to kill him as he entered the hall of judgment. Fortunately, the son of Paul's sister found out about this conspiracy and came to the fortress to inform his uncle of the plot. Probably by this point Paul was not kept under strict guard, because he was an admitted Roman citizen, and his relatives could easily visit him. He would be imprisoned with the same limited freedom both in Caesaria (24:23) and Rome itself (28:16). Desiring to leave the plot a secret, the apostle said nothing to the centurion guarding him, but asked him to bring his nephew directly to the commander. Lysias calmly listened to Paul's nephew and told him not to tell anyone that he had warned the Romans about the plot.

Then Lysias called two centurions to himself and ordered them to prepare a convoy of two hundred soldiers, lightly armed, by nine o'clock in the evening, to take Paul to the Roman governor in Caesaria. Evidently, the commander feared an explosion of fanaticism against Paul, because they could have easily prepared an ambush of dagger-bearing zealots who could overwhelm a smaller convoy. This was a wise and prudent step on the part of the commander, ensuring that Paul, a Roman citizen, would arrive unharmed before the procurator. He also commanded that they prepare donkeys for Paul's comfort during the journey. All this makes it clear that Lysias took care of Paul, probably because he had come to respect him after all that had occurred.

Paul Is Sent to Caesaria to the Procurator Felix (23:23–35).

Marcus Antonius Felix, the procurator of the province of Judea at that time, was the younger brother of Nero's favorite, Pallas, a Greek man freed by Claudius. He was also the son-in-law of Herod Agrippa I. He received his position from

Emperor Claudius after a petition by his brother, around A.D. 53. Tacitus said that he "exercised the power of a king in the spirit of a slave,"[30] and eventually was called back by Nero. However, despite the many justified complaints of the Jews, he never lost the emperor's favor.

Lysias wrote a letter of introduction to Felix, apprising him of Paul's situation, the circumstances of his imprisonment, his status as a Roman citizen, and his political innocence. The convoy led Paul during the night for his safety to Antipatris, a city built by Herod I and named in honor of his father Antipater, located forty-two miles from Jerusalem and another twenty-six miles short of Caesaria. Here, there was no impending danger from the Jews, and the foot soldiers, leaving Paul to the care of the horsemen, returned to Jerusalem. The leader of the convoy, after their arrival in Caesaria, gave Lysias's letter to the procurator and presented Paul to him.

The procurator, having read the letter, asked Paul from what region he hailed, and when he found out that Paul was born in Cilicia, he said that he would hear him when his accusers would arrive. In the meantime, "he commanded him to be kept in Herod's Praetorium," that is, not in the city jail, but in the same palace—built by Herod the Great—in which the procurators themselves lived. This was probably a result of Lysias's positive recommendation.

Acts Chapter Twenty-Four

The Apostle Paul Before the Judgment of the Procurator Felix (24:1–9). Paul's Defense (24:10–21). The Delayed Decision (24:22–23). Paul's Discussion with Felix and Drusilla. The Arrival of a New Procurator (24:24–27).

The Apostle Paul Before the Judgment of the Procurator Felix (24:1–9).

Felix had already been governor of Judea for around seven years by the time Paul arrived, and he left behind him nothing but bad feelings. Being a freedman and a favorite of Claudius, he performed his duties as a ruler with the soul of a slave, abandoning himself to unheard-of debauchery and cruelty. Such a man was to judge the fate of the great apostle of the nations. Five days after Paul's arrival, the high priest Ananias, together with the elders—probably a few chosen members of the Sanhedrin—departed to Caesaria to bring a formal complaint against Paul. They brought with them "a certain orator named Tertullus," whose responsibility it was to give evidence against Paul. Tertullus is a diminutive of the Roman name Tertius. We may assume that this was a Jew of the Diaspora who also had a Roman name, for it is hardly likely that the Sanhedrin would decide to bring an unclean Gentile to speak on their behalf.

He was an orator in the more specific meaning of the word, that is, he was trained both in oratory and in law. Such orators, or rhetors, were numerous in Rome and in the provinces. To incline the governor to his position, Tertullus began his speech with base flattery, saying that the Jews always and everywhere admitted that they were beholden only to Felix for the peace and prosperity of their country. This flattery was obviously a lie, because as soon as Felix was recalled by the emperor, the Jews took advantage to formally lodge complaints about his inept rule. Then Tertullus described Paul as "a plague, a creator of dissension among all the Jews throughout the world, and a ringleader of the sect of the Nazarenes. He even tried to profane the temple, and we seized him, and wanted to judge him according to our law." Here again, Tertullus openly lied, because the Jews had no intention of judging Paul, but they were about to simply murder him in the streets. Lysias's interference he also interprets falsely, as though it were unlawful, because Paul's judgment concerned the Sanhedrin alone. The orator concluded his speech insisting that Paul himself was not able to deny any of the accusations laid at his door. The members of the Sanhedrin immediately confirmed that everything was exactly as Tertullus said.

Paul's Defense (24:10–21).

Paul answered these accusations with dignity. In his speech, we see his natural oratory, the absence of any obsequiousness—although he gave due respect to the person of the governor as the representative of the lawful authority—and, most important, his living faith, his ardent and pure zeal that caused him to forget his self-interest and to think only of the salvation of others. "Inasmuch as I know that you have been for many years a *just* judge of this nation"—there is no flattery in these words, especially because the word "just" is added in the Church Slavonic translation and is not found in the Greek critical text of the Acts. Even if the Church Slavonic reflects the legitimate variant reading of 24:10, all that Paul does is acknowledge that Felix has for a long time been a judge of the nation, and so he knows the customs, habits, and national character of the Jews, and he is well acquainted with the Sanhedrin. Therefore, Paul will defend himself freely, because he knows that this ruler, thanks to his experience of judging the Jews, can accurately determine Paul's innocence.

After this introduction, St Paul said that he came to Jerusalem no more than twelve days before to worship at the temple. No one saw him disputing with anyone, neither in the temple nor in the local synagogues, nor did anyone witness him stirring up mobs in the city streets. Consequently, the accusation that he started riots in Jerusalem was simply a lie, and the accusers had no proof of its truth. At the same time, Paul boldly admitted that he confessed the teaching that his enemies called a heresy. Summarizing the essence of the Christian teaching, Paul forcefully and insistently showed the unity of the New Testament with the Old: "I worship the God of my fathers, believing all thing which are written in the Law and in the Prophets." In other words, Paul said that his worship of God was not a falling away from the religion of his fathers and the Jewish nation, but rather that he serves that same God Whom his accusers also worship. As proof of his words, the apostle said that he and his enemies both hoped for the resurrection of the dead.

This time, the members of the Sanhedrin were more in control of their emotions than they were before Lysias. They recognized how weak their position would look, should their internal divisions be made obvious, as before. Therefore, the Sadducees remained silent this time. While confessing the Christian faith, Paul tried to keep his conscience pure with respect both to God and people, and thus the accusation that he belonged to the Christian faith was not in essence an accusation at all, as being a Christian was not against the Law.

Finally, the apostle defended himself against the last accusation: that he allegedly tried to defile the temple. It is likely that four years had passed since Paul was last in Jerusalem, which is why he expressed himself thus: "now after many years I came to bring alms and offerings to my nation." The purpose of his visit was to bring aid to his people and to worship the True God in His temple by bringing Him a lawful sacrifice. His purpose was in no way to stir up the people. And not only did he not defile the temple, but he entered it according to the laws of ritual purity, not leading a loud mob. Those who seized him were not the ones present before Felix, he said, but "some Jews from Asia," and it should be they who bring formal accusation against him. However, they had nothing to accuse him of, and so they did not come.

In conclusion, the Apostle Paul demanded that his accusers, who had no shred of proof for any of the accusations heaped on him, would at least say, "if they found any wrongdoing in me while I stood before the council," that is, the Sanhedrin, "unless it is for this one statement which I cried out, standing among the them, 'Concerning the resurrection of the dead I am being judged by you this day.'" The irony of Paul's words is profound.

The Delayed Decision (24:22–23).

Felix understood the religious nature of the accusations, the more so because he could not fail to know of Christianity. After all, he lived in Caesaria, where Cornelius the centurion had accepted baptism. Felix refused to give an immediate decision. However, he had no desire to irritate the Sanhedrin, and so he did not free Paul completely, but only delayed his final decision until Lysias should come and give evidence. Paul's imprisonment was mild, and all of his friends could visit him and listen to him preach.

Paul's Discussion with Felix and Drusilla. The Arrival of a New Procurator (24:24–27).

Some time later, Felix and his wife Drusilla—who was Jewish and could give him counsel about the matter—called Paul to himself and heard him preach the Christian faith. This Drusilla was the daughter of Herod Agrippa I, who killed James. She was a renowned beauty in Caesaria. Of course, Felix himself was interested in Paul, but most likely Drusilla was the one who insisted on seeing and hearing one of the most famous preachers of Christianity. Paul spoke to Felix and his wife not only about things they wanted to hear, but also about things they did not want to hear, things that Paul considered it his duty to speak of: "about righteousness, self-control, and the judgment to come." His words were so effective that the cruel and dissolute Felix (Tacitus wrote that he allowed himself all manner of injustice and immoderation and "he perpetrated all sorts of villainy without fear of punishment") was afraid, and he sent Paul away, promising to speak with him later.

We easily can see what sort of a man Felix was in his hope "that money would be given him by Paul, that he might release him. Therefore, he sent for him more often and conversed with him." Doubtless knowing that local Christians were taking a great interest in the fate of the prisoner, he was hoping that they would give him a large bribe. Thus, he kept him imprisoned for two years.

In A.D. 60 or 61, Felix was removed from his position and replaced by Porcius Festus. Little is known about this man, and the little we know is positive. He ruled a short time and died in the following year, replaced by Lucceius Albinus. Desiring to be well remembered by the Jews, Felix never did release Paul, even though he apparently considered him innocent. Paul remained in bonds, officially considered under trial.

Acts Chapter Twenty-Five

Procurator Festus in Jerusalem, and Official Complaints About Paul by the Jews (25:1–6). The Trial Before Festus (25:7–12). King Agrippa II and Bernice in Caesaria. Their Desire to Hear the Apostle Paul (25:13–27).

Procurator Festus in Jerusalem, and Official Complaints About Paul by the Jews (25:1-6).

Having begun his rule, Festus traveled to Jerusalem, and immediately upon his arrival the high priest and "chief men of the Jews" came to him with a formal complaint against Paul, asking him to send Paul to Jerusalem, obviously with the same intention of killing him along the way. The high priest at that point was Ishmael ben Fabus, whom Festus himself had appointed in place of Ananias. Festus was wise enough not to listen to their request and refused to send Paul to them. He told them that Paul was to remain under guard in Caesaria, and he himself would be returning there shortly, so there was no need to send for the prisoner to travel to Jerusalem. Instead, he offered "those who have authority among you" to come to Caesaria to accuse Paul formally. This they agreed to do.

The Trial Before Festus (25:7–12).

"When he had remained among them more than ten days," Festus returned to his residence in Caesaria, and on the next day, he began Paul's trial. His accusers were already present and began to accuse him of many things, none of which they could prove. From Paul's answer in verse 8 it is clear that these were all the same accusations as before, but there was one new one: some crime against Caesar, something like the slander of the Thessalonian Jews against Paul, who insisted that Paul considered Jesus to be the only rightful king and taught others the same (Acts 17:6). Paul firmly denied this accusation, saying that he never transgressed the Law of the Jews, the ritual purity of the temple, or Roman Law.

Then Festus, desiring to please the Jews, asked Paul, "Are you willing to go up to Jerusalem and there be judged before me concerning these things?" This question could have two meanings: "Do you want to go to Jerusalem so that I, as a judge, can give my decision there in the presence of the Sanhedrin?" or "There the Sanhedrin will judge you in my presence." In the first case, Paul would be judged by Roman Law as a Roman citizen of Jewish birth. In the second case, Paul would be judged by national Jewish Law, as long as it did not contradict Roman Law.

Paul appreciated the danger of this turn of events, and he firmly refused this suggestion of the procurator, saying, "To the Jews I have done no wrong, as you very well know." Therefore, he had no desire to be once again judged by the Sanhedrin. Since, in the person of the procurator, he effectively stood before the judgment of Caesar (the governor judged in Caesar's name), Paul appealed directly to Caesar to avoid the prejudiced justice of the Jews. In addition, he said that he was ready to die if he had done anything worthy of death. From these words, it is obvious that Paul did not expect fair judgment either from the Jews or from Festus, because Festus was obviously more interested in doing the Jews a favor.

Doubtless Paul's appeal to Caesar was inspired by Christ's own words in the vision, in which He told Paul that he would preach in Rome (23:11). Now the circumstances were favorable for his journey to Rome, for every Roman citizen had the right of appeal before Caesar's person. These words ended the formal proceedings. After Festus conferred with the council concerning Paul's right to appeal, Festus announced, "You have appealed to Caesar? To Caesar you shall go!" It seems the procurator was displeased with Paul, which is understandable given Paul's rather forceful words in 25:10–11.

King Agrippa II and Bernice in Caesaria. Their Desire to Hear the Apostle Paul (25:13–27).

A few days later, King Herod Agrippa II and his sister Bernice arrived in Caesaria to congratulate Festus on his accession to the governorship. Agrippa II was the last king of the line of Herod, the son of Agrippa I (see Acts 12), the great-grandson of Herod the Great, and the brother of Drusilla (Felix's wife). He was raised in the court of Emperor Claudius, who gave him the small Syrian kingdom of Chalcis soon after his father's death, and four years after that (ca. A.D. 53), Claudius gave him the entire tetrarchy of Philip and Lysanias with the title of "king" and the authority over the temple in Jerusalem (which was finally rebuilt during his reign). He also gave him the right to choose high priests.

Bernice was his sister, previously married to her uncle Herod, but now (according to Josephus) living in an incestuous union with her brother. Later she married the Cilician king Polemon II, whom she abandoned for Vespasian and Titus. Because Agrippa was a client king of Rome, he considered it his duty to greet the new procurator. Considering Agrippa to be an expert in all Jewish affairs, Festus gave him a detailed account of Paul's case. This inspired in Agrippa a desire to see and listen to the famous prisoner, whom all the Jews hated and yet the Roman governor considered innocent. It is likely that Agrippa had heard of Paul and Christianity before, as did Bernice, and now they were pleased to have the opportunity to see and hear one of the most important preachers of the new faith.

This desire of the honored guest was fulfilled the next day. Agrippa and Bernice, arrayed in royal finery, entered the hall of judgment with the "commanders and the prominent men of the city." Caesaria, as the residence of the Roman governor, had five cohorts of Roman troops, with five commanders. This whole affair was filled with great pomp, because the high society of Caesaria was all in attendance, and the apostle was brought into such a brilliant assembly in bonds (see 26:29). Introducing the prisoner to those assembled, Festus explained why he brought him before them, saying that he was convinced that Paul had done nothing worthy of death according to Roman Law, but he "had nothing certain to write to my lord concerning him," and so he offered all those present to listen to Paul and come to their own conclusions about the matter, especially King Agrippa, as one well versed with local custom. With their help, Festus would then be better able to write a letter of recommendation to Emperor Nero.

Acts Chapter Twenty-Six

Paul's Defense Before Festus, Agrippa, and Others with a Summary of His Life and Conversion to Christ (26:1–27). The Opinion of Agrippa and the Others Concerning Paul's Case: They Admit His Innocence (26:28–32).

Paul's Defense Before Festus, Agrippa, and Others with a Summary of His Life and Conversion to Christ (26:1–27).

Agrippa, as king and honored guest of the procurator, chaired the meeting, opening and formally concluding it. However, as one raised in the Roman court, he officially began the proceedings not by addressing Paul with the words "I command you," but with the words "You are permitted to speak for yourself," out of deference for the authority of the governor. Then Paul, stretching out his hand, not as a request for silence (as in 12:17 and 13:16), but for the sake of the majesty of the moment, began to speak. This speech is wonderful because it is not so much a personal defense as a defense of his ministry—the preaching of Christianity, to which he was called. This is the last triumphant witness of the Holy Apostle Paul concerning Christ in the Holy Land of Palestine, uttered before the most honored representatives of the Jewish and pagan nations, who were fated to become one flock under the guidance of the One Shepherd.

The apostle began his speech with an address to the king with the same dignity with which he had addressed Felix not long before. He expressed joy that he had been given such an opportunity to defend his ministry before a king who knew all the customs and opinions of the Jews. Consequently, he was more qualified to judge his innocence even better than the others, including the procurator. Paul began the actual defense by referring to the witness of those who knew him even before his conversion to Christianity. He indicated that from his earliest years, he was educated not in Tarsus, but in Jerusalem, where he was probably brought as a small child to learn the Law of God. He lived as a Pharisee, in full agreement with the requirements of this strictest and most conservative sect of Judaism.

Then Paul spoke of his current position as prisoner, and said that it was not for betraying his previous convictions that he was judged worthy of death by the Jews, but only because he, like all Jews, hoped to see the coming of the kingdom of the Messiah, promised by God to the ancestors of the Jews and awaited by the whole nation. The Jews were especially irritated by Paul's placing the resurrection of Jesus of Nazareth as the foundation for his teaching concerning the coming of the kingdom of the Messiah. This is why he said, "Why should it be thought incredible by you that God raises the dead?"

Then Paul admitted that he used to be a cruel persecutor of those who believed in Jesus of Nazareth, Who rose from the dead and is the promised Messiah. He then told in detail of his conversion to Christ on the road to Damascus, in a manner similar to his defense before the mob in Jerusalem (Acts 22). In this particular account, he mentions some details that seem to diverge from the previous two accounts, but in general, this is essentially the same account. The most important detail in this version is a more specific account of the Lord's words to Saul, in which the Lord revealed to him the purpose of His appearance—to make Saul his servant and witness, equal to the rest of the apostles. Notably, the Lord, according to Paul, Himself promised to appear to His newly chosen witness and to reveal His will to him directly, which we see repeatedly from the narrative of Paul's mission (22:17, 23:11, and others).

"I will deliver you from the Jewish people, as well as from the Gentiles." This is something we hear again and again in Paul's ministry, especially when he was repeatedly saved from fatal danger. From the words of the Lord, it is clear that it was His will for Paul to first preach to the Jews in any given city, and only then to the Gentiles. The Lord also explained to Paul the purpose of his calling: "to open their eyes, in order to turn them from darkness to light," to open their spiritual eyes to the knowledge of God's truth, "that they may receive forgiveness of sins and an inheritance among those who are sanctified by faith" in the Lord Jesus Christ as the Messiah.

Then the apostle explained that he could not oppose the heavenly vision, and so he began to preach first to the Jews in Damascus and Jerusalem and in the entire land of Judea, and only later to the pagans. For this, the Jews seized him in the temple and wanted to kill him, but God helped him, and he remained alive to this day, preaching to the insignificant and the great, and never in any way deviating from the prophecies of Moses and the prophets, that is, that Christ had to die and, having been the first to rise from the dead, "would proclaim light to the Jewish people and to the Gentiles."

Here the energetic and powerful speech was interrupted by the frivolous, impetuous, and curt voice of the procurator: "Paul, you are beside yourself! Much learning is driving you mad!" Just as Pilate considered Christ's truth revealed on earth to be an empty delusion, so now Festus, the pagan, considered Paul's ardent words to be madness. Paul answered with great dignity, "I am not mad, most noble Festus, but speak the words of truth and reason." To instruct this pagan who understood so little, St Paul referred to Agrippa as one who "knows these things," and to whom, for the most part, Paul's speech was directed in the first place. The apostle said that he did not believe that any "of these things," that is, the life and ministry of Jesus Christ, "escapes his attention, since this thing was not done in a corner," that is, in secret, but before the eyes of the entire Jewish nation both in Jerusalem and in all of Palestine.

The Opinion of Agrippa and the Others Concerning Paul's Case: They Admit His Innocence (26:28–32).

With a decisive and unexpected turn of phrase, Paul suddenly spoke directly to the conscience of Agrippa and, as an experienced "fisher of men," nearly caught him. Only the king's frivolity prevented him from being caught, but he hurried to end the tribunal after these words, from which we can clearly deduce that something stirred in his conscience.

"King Agrippa, do you believe the prophets?" unexpectedly asked Paul and immediately answered his own question: "I know that you do believe." Although raised at the court of the Roman emperor, Agrippa probably remained a Jew at heart. The completion of the renovation of the temple during his reign (which had begun under Herod the Great, his great-grandfather) is proof that to some degree, even if in the farthest depths of his soul, Agrippa had a sense of Jewish religiosity. The piercing gaze of the Apostle Paul saw this and so keenly awoke this religious sense that the king was confused, especially considering the circumstances—he was in the presence of the Roman governor, who doubtless considered him a Roman fosterling above all such "Jewish superstitions." This newly inspired sense was put down fiercely by fear and shame before the educated Roman elite, and Agrippa turned it into hypocrisy and profane sarcasm, and mocking, he said, "You almost persuade me to become a Christian."

In answer to the cutting sarcasm, Paul answered in an inspired and moving manner: "I would to God that not only you, but also all who hear me today, might become both almost and altogether such as I am, except for these chains." Paul's chains were his glory (Eph 3:1, 4:1; Phlm 1; Phil 2:17), but of course, he could not desire that all Christians always would be in chains. Paul's inspired answer once again awoke King Agrippa's conscience, and he, no longer in a fit state to listen to him calmly, quickly ended the proceedings. Paul's speech was a superlative example of dignity, freedom, and love, and this could not help but make an impression on impartial listeners. Having conferred among themselves, the king and the others agreed that Paul should be freed from his chains, an innocent man, but because Paul already had appealed to Caesar, Festus decided to send him to Rome.

Acts Chapter Twenty-Seven

Paul's Journey from Caesaria to Rome. From Caesaria to Myra in Lycia (27:1–5). From Myra to Crete and Paul's Warning, Which Was Not Heeded (27:6–13). A Fierce Storm from Crete to Malta, the Wreck of the Ship, the Salvation of the Passengers by Swimming Ashore (27:14–44).

Paul's Journey from Caesaria to Rome. From Caesaria to Myra in Lycia (27:1–5). "When it was decided that we should sail to Italy," which occurred in the autumn of A.D. 61, the Apostle Paul, together was some other prisoners, was committed to the centurion Julius, who commanded the Augustan Regiment. As in obvious from the use of the first person plural, St Luke was from this moment again a fellow traveler of St Paul. From verse 2, we see that Paul's other fellow traveler was Aristarchus, a Macedonian of Thessalonica. What the Augustan Regiment is cannot be determined; it is possible that this was a division of Nero's personal cavalry that for some reason was in the East and now returned to Rome, something that Festus took advantage of to transport the prisoners to their trials before Caesar.

Because there was no Rome-bound ship in Caesaria, the prisoners were taken on a merchant vessel bound for Adramyttium, a coastal city in Misia, Asia Minor, not far from Troas. This was done with the intention of finding a ship bound for Rome in one of the cities along the trade route, and this was exactly what happened. On the next day they landed at Sidon, the ancient trading city in Phoenicia. Treating Paul with respect, Julius allowed him to leave the ship to visit his friends and "receive care," that is, necessities for his journey. Julius probably treated Paul well as a result of Festus's direct command; however, it is also possible that Paul's personality won him over. Because of contrary winds, their ship went off course and landed on Cyprus. Later they had to sail along the coast of Cilicia and Pamphylia, to enter the harbor of Myra in Lycia. This was a flourishing city several miles from the sea along a river that could easily bear ships all the way to the city.

From Myra to Crete and Paul's Warning, Which Was Not Heeded (27:6–13).
Here in Myra the centurion found an Alexandrian ship that was just about to raise anchor to sail to Italy. He put the prisoners and the division of soldiers on board. Most likely, this ship was also a merchant vessel, because it was laden with wheat (v. 38), but why it was in Asia Minor is not clear. Alexandria and Egypt were the breadbasket of Italy, so to speak, and so trade between the two was vigorous, but why this ship did not go directly from Alexandria to Italy is difficult to say. Perhaps contrary winds turned it away from a direct path, or perhaps trade with Asia Minor. It was evidently a very large ship, for it could fit 276 people in addition to trade wares (see v. 37). Because of a contrary wind, they sailed very slowly and only after several days (instead of the usual single day), they reached Cnidus, a city in the Asian province of Caria, but the wind prevented their landing. Then they managed to sail to Crete off Salmone.

"Passing it with difficulty," the ship sailed around the eastern side of the island and entered a bay on the southern side, called "Fair Havens," near the city of Lasea. This harbor was well protected from the northwestern winds that were contrary to the ship's course, hindering it and forcing it to remain in the harbor. A long time had passed from the beginning of the journey, and "the Fast was already over." This fast is doubtless the Day of Atonement (Yom Kippur), usually falling in late September or early October. Consequently, this was after the autumnal equinox, when sailing at sea, especially in those places, could be very dangerous.

The Apostle Paul, based on his previous experience of sailing the Mediterranean (2 Cor 11:25), warned them not to try to continue the journey, because it was dangerous not only for the trade goods but for the passengers as well. But the centurion trusted the helmsman and the captain, naturally considering them more experienced than Paul, and as the Fair Havens were not a good place to winter, they decided to try to reach Phoenix, another harbor on the southern side of Crete that was protected from both southwest and northwest winds, and so was a better place to winter. Because a south wind blew, they decided that now was a good time to try to reach Phoenix, for the south wind did not threaten to push them out to sea.

A Fierce Storm from Crete to Malta, the Wreck of the Ship, the Salvation of the Passengers by Swimming Ashore (27:14–44).
However, the ship's captain was mistaken in his assumptions. Suddenly a southeast wind rose, called Euroclydon, which did not allow them to approach Phoenix, but pushed them out into open sea. Powerless against the wind, the sailors allowed the ship to be carried by the wind. Then the ship sailed by a small island called Clauda, southwest from Lasea and Fair Havens, and they "secured the skiff with

difficulty." Having raised the skiff, they began to tie down the ship with cables and ropes, lest the wind tear the ship apart, and they lowered the sails to prevent the ship from going too fast and capsizing on the reefs along the African coast, not far east from Tripoli (called the "Syrtis Sands"). Because the wind showed no signs of abating, they began to throw out the trade goods to lighten the ship, and then the tackle on the third day.

Their situation was becoming dire, and soon all hope seemed lost. For many days, they saw neither the sun, nor stars, and could not even determine where they were going (the compass had not yet been invented). The despairing passengers had even stopped eating, and then St Paul began to encourage everyone, inspiring in them a spirit of endurance and hope in deliverance. Meekly rebuking them for not listening to his warning, he encouraged them by telling of an appearance of an angel of God, who said to him, "Do not be afraid Paul; you must be brought before Caesar; and indeed God has granted you all those who sail with you." To further convince them, Paul insisted on his own conviction that everything would be as the angel said and that they would be cast out on some island. On the fourteenth night after their departure from Fair Havens, the sailors began to guess that they were approaching land.

Here St Luke says that they sailed in the Adriatic Sea, but if one looks at a modern map, the body of water is clearly the Ionian Sea. In ancient times, the entire area between Greece and southern Italy and Sicily was called the Adriatic Sea, including the island of Malta. The sailors began to measure the depth of the sea, and it turned out to be twenty fathoms, then fifteen soon afterward, which meant that land was near and there was a danger of running aground on shallow rocks near small islands. "They dropped four anchors from the stern" to secure the boat in place, and began to await the coming of day. The frightened sailors wanted to take advantage of the darkness to escape on the skiff, leaving the prisoners to their fate. The Apostle Paul understood their intent and warned the centurion that if the sailors left, everyone would die, because none of the passengers could navigate a ship.

Paul's words were characteristic: "you cannot be saved." He said "you" because he was completely sure of his own salvation. The soldiers cut off the ropes that attached the skiff, and it fell and was carried away by the waves. Before the break of day, Paul once again began to encourage his fellow travelers with the hope of deliverance and convinced them all to eat some food, leading by example, thanking God before all. Having strengthened themselves with food, they all once again began to lighten the ship by throwing out the wheat, for 276 passengers alone were a great weight. When day finally came, they could not determine what the island was, but they saw a bay with a beach, and they tried to steer the ship into harbor.

They raised the anchors and "left them in the sea, meanwhile loosing the rudder ropes," which usually are tied during storms and at anchorage for the safety of the rudder, "and they hoisted the mainsail to the wind and made for shore" slowly and carefully. However, the ship ran aground, "and the prow stuck fast and remained immovable, but the stern was being broken up by the violence of the waves." Then the soldiers wanted to kill all the prisoners, lest any of them escape, but the centurion, desiring to keep Paul alive, stopped them, probably because of his own respect for Paul, or maybe because of orders from Festus. He found another way of preventing the prisoners from escaping. He "commanded that those [soldiers] who could swim should jump overboard first and get to land," and thus those first arriving on land would be the guard that could prevent any of the prisoners from escaping. The rest either swam or came in with the flotsam. All were saved.

Acts Chapter Twenty-Eight

The Continuation of St Paul's Journey to Rome. The Hospitality of the Natives on Malta. The Viper That Caused Paul No Harm. Paul's Healing of Many Sick on the Island and the Continuation of the Journey (28:1–14). Arrival in Rome (28:15–16). Paul's Twofold Conversation with the Jews in Rome (28:17–29). The Conclusion of the Book of the Acts of the Apostles (28:30–31).

The Continuation of St Paul's Journey to Rome. The Hospitality of the Natives on Malta. The Viper That Caused Paul No Harm. Paul's Healing of Many Sick on the Island and the Continuation of the Journey (28:1–14).

The survivors found out from the natives that the island was called Malta. Some ancient commentators thought that this small island was actually in the Adriatic as we know it today, near the Dalmatian shores and Ragusa (today's Dubrovnik), but the problem with this interpretation is that such terrible storms do not occur in the Adriatic, and the ship was carried from Crete by a northeast wind, which is why it could not go north. Finally, the closest way to Rome from Dubrovnik is not via Sicily. More recent scholars are nearly unanimous in agreement that the island where they landed is Malta (Melite in Greek), an island fifteen miles south of Sicily, nearly fifty miles from Africa. It is plausible that the ship bearing Paul could have reached Malta from Crete by a stormy northeast wind. The most direct way to Rome from Malta is indeed via Sicily as is described in verses 12–13. In addition, local Maltese tradition preserves a story of Paul's visit that closely corresponds to the account in Acts.

The natives (literally "barbarians," meaning those not of Greek or Roman origin) of Malta were probably of Punic extraction (i.e., Phoenicio-Carthaginian). They showed the survivors warm hospitality by lighting fires to warm them, as it was raining and cold. When Paul had gathered much wood and thrown it into the fire, a viper that had been inactive because of the cold suddenly came to life with the warmth of the fire and bit Paul in the hand. The natives, seeing that the viper was poisonous, were sure that he would presently die. They began to suspect that he was probably a killer, because God's justice did not allow him to enjoy his deliverance from death at sea. However, when they saw that he simply threw the snake into the fire, having suffered no harm from it, they began to say that he was a god, that is, one of the gods who had taken human form.

Currently, there are no poisonous snakes on Malta, and the locals have a tradition that after St Paul threw the viper into the fire, all the members of that species ceased to be poisonous. The "leading citizen of the island," named Publius, had an estate nearby and invited Paul and his fellow travelers (Luke and Aristarchus, not all 276 passengers, as we see in verse 10) to his home, where he took care of them for three days. Here Paul miraculously healed Publius's father of fever and dysentery, after which many others on the island began to bring their sick to him, and he healed them all. Their gratitude was great, and they honored Paul and his fellow travelers in many ways and "provided such things as were necessary" for the rest of the journey to Rome.

After three months on Malta, when stormy autumn and most of winter had passed, making further sailing no longer dangerous, they sailed on another Alexandrian ship with a figurehead of the Twin Brothers, Castor and Pollux, the mythological heroes who were considered protectors against storms. The ship had wintered in Syracuse, a coastal Sicilian town eighteen miles away from Malta. From Malta, the ship returned to Syracuse for three days, and then sailed to Rhegium (Reggio Calabria today) in southern Italy, opposite Messina. With a good wind, they quickly reached Puteoli on the next day (Pozzuoli near Naples). At that time, the harbor of Puteoli was one of the most important ports on the western shore of Italy, especially for trade with the East. Most trade vessels disembarked here, and their wares traveled the rest of the way by land to Rome, the capital of the civilized world.

The rest of the apostle's journey should have gone by foot. But in Puteoli, Paul found Christians who asked Paul and his fellow travelers to remain with them, and they did so for seven days. This shows what great trust Julius placed in Paul, leaving him with only a small convoy, whereas the rest of the prisoners traveled with Julius himself to Rome. Seven days later, Paul, Luke, and Aristarchus traveled to Rome along the famous Appian Way.

Arrival in Rome (28:15–16).

Many Roman Christians, having learned of the great apostle's arrival, hurried to meet him "as far as Appii Forum," a small town about forty miles south of Rome, "and Three Inns," about ten miles from Rome. "When Paul saw them, he thanked God and took courage." In this solicitude of the Roman brethren, he saw a pledge that his bonds would not be a great barrier to his apostolic ministry in Rome. Thus did Paul's long-lived desire to visit the great capital of the world come to pass.

The prisoners were delivered to the captain of the guard after arriving in Rome. This captain was one of the prefects of the Praetorian Guard, whose responsibility included accepting and guarding people who had appealed to Caesar. Paul was given an exception: he was permitted to live by himself, separated from the rest of the prisoners, alone and with relative freedom, under a single guard who was also probably a Praetorian. Again, such preferential treatment was probably a result of the positive recommendations of both Festus and Julius. Paul was allowed to leave his place of residence (as long as his guard accompanied him), to receive visitors, and to send letters. He used this limited freedom for his apostolic ministry.

Paul's Twofold Conversation with the Jews in Rome and the Conclusion of the Book of Acts (28:17–31).

Three days after his arrival in Rome, Paul called the most well-known Jews in Rome to himself and told them that he had never done anything against his nation or against the customs that they kept from their fathers. He was seized in Jerusalem and committed to the justice of the Roman authority in Caesaria, and after the procurator investigated his case, he had wanted to free him, but since the local Jews opposed this, Paul had no other recourse except to demand trial before Caesar. Still, he had no intention of accusing his people of anything before Caesar.

Thus, Paul followed his own custom and began his preaching in Rome with the Jews. Because he, a prisoner, did not have the freedom to visit the local synagogue, he invited them to visit him, and began with this self-justification to explain to them why he was imprisoned. This explanation became the motive for the beginning of his preaching of Christ: "for the hope of Israel I am bound with this chain."

The Jews answered Paul that they had received no letters about him from Jerusalem, and no one had given them a negative recommendation, even by word of mouth. However, they had heard that Christianity was "a sect" that was disputed everywhere, and they would themselves like to hear of it from his own lips. On a day they suggested, Paul was visited not only by the elites, but by many other local Jews who desired to hear him. From morning to evening, he taught them concerning the kingdom of God, that is, the Christian faith, providing them with proofs from the Prophets concerning Christ Jesus as the Messiah promised by the Law of Moses and the prophecies of the Old Testament.

Some believed him; others did not. They were about to leave, arguing among themselves, when Paul took the opportunity to remind them of the threatening words of Isaiah the prophet, who foretold Israel's stubbornness and lack of faith in chapter 6, verses 9–10. Paul concluded his preaching by telling them that the salvation of God would be offered to the pagans, and the pagans would listen.

The Acts of the Apostles conclude with a testimony concerning Paul's two-year stay in Rome. He lived "in his own rented house," accepting all who came to him, "preaching the kingdom of God and teaching the things which concern the Lord Jesus Christ with all confidence, no one forbidding him." Evidently, during that time, he was supported by the local Roman Christians, and two years later he was released. From Rome, Paul wrote his Epistles to the Philippians, Ephesians, Colossians, Philemon, and the Hebrews. The abrupt ending of the Book of Acts at the most interesting moment—Paul's imminent trial before Caesar—proves its authenticity, and that it was written during that time, before Paul's second imprisonment in Rome and his subsequent martyrdom in A.D. 67.

Sources

This series, *Commentary on the Holy Scriptures of the New Testament*, is a summary of the course taught by Archbishop Averky at Holy Trinity Seminary between 1951 and 1953. The complete work provides a synthesis of various pre-Revolutionary works and textbooks on the Holy Scriptures of the New Testament which were published in Russia and used both as a means for self-education and as part of the curricula of our various theological academies and seminaries. The sources listed were either used by Archbishop Averky when writing this work or cited by the editor within this volume.

Alexandrov, Fr N. *A Manual for Studying the Holy Books of the New Testament* [in Russian].

Barsov, M. *A Collection of Articles on Exegetical and Instructive Reading of the Acts of the Apostles* [in Russian].

Bishop Michael. *The Annotated Epistles*, including the Acts and the General Epistles [in Russian].

Blessed Theophylact. *Exposition on the Acts of the Holy Apostles* 1:2, *Patrologia Graec* [PG].

Gill, Joseph, ed. *Concilium Florentinum: documenta et scriptores*. Vol. 5, Fasc. 2, Part 2. Rome: Pontificium Institutum Orientalium Studiorum, 1953.

Glover, T. R. In *Tertullian, Minucius Felix.* Loeb Classical Library 250. Cambridge, MA: Harvard University Press; London: Heinemann, 1977.

Ivanov, I. V. *A Handbook for Studying the Holy Books of the New Testament* [in Russian].

Josephus, Flavius. *Josephus, the Essential Works: A Condensation of Jewish Antiquities and The Jewish War*, trans. and ed. Paul L. Maier. Grand Rapids, MI: Kregel Publications, 1994.

Kheraskov, Fr Michael. *An Exegetical Summary of the Holy Books of the New Testament* [in Russian].

Lambertsen, Isaac, trans. *The Pentecostarion of the Orthodox Church*. Liberty, TN: Saint John of Kronstadt Press, 2007.

Roberts, Alexander, and James Donaldson, eds. *The Ante-Nicene Fathers* [ANF]. 1885–1887. 10 vols. Repr. Peabody, MA: Hendrickson, 1994.

St Dimitry of Rostov. *Cheti Minei* [in Russian].

St Gregory the Theologian. *Oration 41 on Pentecost*; ET *Festal Orations*, trans. N. V. Harrison Crestwood, NY: St Vladimir's Seminary Press, 2008.

St John Chrysostom. *Homilies on the Acts of the Apostles* 3.1. ET in *Nicene and Post-Nicene Fathers* [NPNF].

St Theophan the Recluse. *Мысли на каждый день года по церковным чтениям из Слова Божия* [Thoughts for Every Day of the Year According to the Ecclesiastical Lessons from the Word of God] [in Russian]. Moscow: Sretensky Monastery/Pravilo Very, 1995.

Tacitus, Cornelius. *The Annals and the Histories of Tacitus.* London: New English Library, 1966.

Notes

Chapter 3

1. Blessed Theophylact, Exposition on the Acts of the Holy Apostles 1:2, Patrologia Graeca (further, PG) 125, col. 504.

2. St John Chrysostom, *Homilies on the Acts of the Apostles* 3.1; ET in *Nicene and Post-Nicene Fathers* (further, NPNF), series 1, vol. 11, p. 18.

3. St Theophan the Recluse, *Мысли на каждый день года по церковным чтениям из Слова Божия* [Thoughts for Every Day of the Year according to the Ecclesiastical Lessons from the Word of God] (Moscow: Sretensky Monastery/Pravilo Very, 1995), 128.

4. Blessed Theophylact, *Exposition in Acts* 2:1–4, PG 125, col. 529D–532A.

5. See St Gregory the Theologian, *Oration 41 on Pentecost*; ET *Festal Orations*, trans. N. V. Harrison (Crestwood, NY: St Vladimir's Seminary Press, 2008), 143–59.

6. *Pentecostarion*, Troparion for the Feast of Pentecost.

7. St John Chrysostom, *Homilies on Acts* 5.2; NPNF, vol. 11, p. 34.

8. St John Chrysostom, *Homilies on Acts* 6.3; NPNF vol. 11, p. 41.

9. See Josephus, *Jewish War* 5.5.4.

10. St John Chrysostom, *Homilies on Acts* 9.3; NPNF vol. 11, p. 58.

11. St John Chrysostom, *Homilies on Acts* 10.2; NPNF vol. 11, p. 65–66.

12. St John Chrysostom, *Homilies on Acts* 11.1; NPNF vol. 11, p. 70.

13. St Dimitry of Rostov, *Cheti Minei*, November 28.

14. Exact quotation: "the blood of Christians is seed"; Tertullian, *Apologeticus* 50.13; ET by T.R. Glover in *Tertullian, Minucius Felix*, Loeb Classical Library 250 (Cambridge, MA: Harvard University Press; London: Heinemann, 1977), 226–27.

15. See St Justin Martyr, *First Apology* 26; ET in *Ante-Nicene Fathers* (further, ANF), vol. 1, p. 171–72.

16. St John Chrysostom, *Homilies on Acts* 18.2; ET in NPNF, vol. 11, p. 115.

17. St Irenaeus of Lyons, *Against the Heresies* 3.12.8; ET in ANF, vol. 1, p. 433.

18. St John Chrysostom, *Homilies on Acts* 20.2; ET in NPNF, vol. 11, p. 131.

19. Ibid., p. 130.

20. For example, "Thus we define that the holy apostolic see and the Roman pontiff has primacy in the whole world, and the Roman pontiff

himself is the successor of blessed Peter, prince of the apostles, and true vicar of Christ, as well as the head of the whole Church and father and teacher of all Christians." – Definition of the Council of Florence of the Roman Catholic Church (1439–1449) in Joseph Gill, ed. *Concilium Florentinum: documenta et scriptores*, vol. 5, fasc. 2, part 2 (Rome: Pontificium Institutum Orientalium Studiorum, 1953), p. 464.

21. St John Chrysostom, *Homilies on Acts* 25.1; ET in NPNF, vol. 11, p. 162.

22. See Josephus, *Antiquities of the Jews* 19.8.2 (see footnote 23 for the full citation of the passage).

23. In an account largely corresponding with Acts 12:20–23, Flavius Josephus describes the death of Herod Agrippa I thus: "On the second day of the spectacles [the king] put on a garment made wholly of silver, of a truly wonderful texture, and came into the theater early in the morning. […] Presently his flatterers cried out … that he was a god, and they added, 'Be thou merciful to us; for although we have hitherto reverenced thee only as a man, yet shall we henceforth own thee as superior to mortal nature.' Upon this the king neither rebuked them nor rejected their impious flattery. But he shortly afterward looked up and saw an owl sitting on a certain rope over his head, and immediately understood that this bird was the messenger of ill tidings, … and fell into the deepest sorrow. A severe pain arose in his belly, striking with a most violent intensity. He therefore looked upon his friends, and said, 'I, whom you call a god, am commanded presently to depart this life; while Providence thus reproves the lying words you just now said to me; and I, who was by you called immortal, am immediately to be hurried away by death. But I am bound to accept what Providence allots, as it pleases God; for we have by no means lived ill, but in a splendid and happy manner.' When he had said this, his pain became violent. […] And when he had been quite worn out by the pain in his belly for five days, he departed this life" (Josephus, *Antiquities of the Jews* 19.8.2).

Chapter 4

24. Blessed Theophylact, *Exposition in Acts* 13:52, PG 125, col. 704C.

25. St John Chrysostom, *Homilies on Acts* 34.2; ET in NPNF, vol. 11, p. 214.

26. Ibid., p. 221.

27. See St John Chrysostom, *Homilies on Acts* 43.1; ET in NPNF, vol. 11, p. 264.

28. Blessed Theophylact, *Exposition in Acts* 20:28, PG vol. 125, col. 780A.

29. This saying of the Lord belongs to the *agrapha* (i.e., "unwritten"), that is, the sayings that are not found in the canonical Gospel accounts.

30. Tacitus, *Histories* 5.9.

Subject Index

Scripture Index

Old Testament

New Testament